Warren Hassmer

12[00]

GENTIANS

GENTIANS

Fritz Köhlein

translated from the German by David Winstanley
edited by Jim Jermyn

CHRISTOPHER HELM
A & C Black · London

TIMBER PRESS
Portland, Oregon

(A translation of the first section of *Enziane und Glockenblumen* (*Gentians and Bellflowers*) by Fritz Köhlein (Verlag Eugen Ulmer, Stuttgart, 1986)

This translation published by Christopher Helm (Publishers) Ltd, Imperial House, 21–25 North Street, Bromley, Kent BR1 1SD, a subsidiary of A & C Black (Publishers) Ltd, 35 Bedford Row, London WC1R 4JH

Drawings by Marlene Gemke, based on preliminary sketches by the author.

ISBN 0 7136-8075-X

A CIP catalogue record for this book is available from the British Library.

First published in North America in 1991 by
Timber Press, Inc.
9999 S.W. Wilshire
Portland, Oregon 97225, USA

ISBN 0-88192-192-0

Phototypesetting by Rowland Phototypesetting Ltd
Bury St Edmunds, Suffolk

Reproduced, printed and bound in Great Britain by
Biddles Ltd, Guildford, Surrey

Contents

Colour Plates

Figures

Foreword and Acknowledgements

I have tried to deal with the theme of gentians from every angle, so that this book may be useful to gardeners, plant-lovers, garden-planners and botanists. Thanks to the worldwide exchange of seed, new species are continually finding their way into cultivation; even seed from short-lived species such as those of *Gentianella* and *Gentianopsis* is offered in some of the recent lists.

So as to provide a comprehensive guide, a wide range of species has been included. It is hoped that this volume may also help to disentangle the confusion caused by the close similarity of many gentian species. Among subjects discussed in some detail are the natural ranges of the species, cultivation, their uses in the garden and the choice of suitable neighbours.

I owe a debt of thanks to my German publisher, Roland Ulmer. I am also deeply indebted to Dr H. C. Fritz Encke, Greifenstein, for his continuing help in problems of nomenclature, and to Dr James S. Pringle of the Royal Botanic Garden, Hamilton, Ontario, a leading expert on the genus *Gentiana*, for his generous support. I also enjoyed help from my correspondent of many years' standing, Mr Michio Cozuca (Japan), from Professor J. Sieber, Weihenstephan (plant trials), Herr Gert Böhme (GDR) in elucidating the nomenclature of various species from the Soviet Union, and to numerous other helpers, here unnamed. For assistance in supplying photographs I am indebted to Herr Wilhelm Schacht (Munich-Nymphenburg) and in particular to my old friend Hermann Fuchs (Hof). It only remains to thank my wife Annemarie once again for her patience and helpfulness.

For the English edition of the book, I would like to thank my translator, Dr David Winstanley, and Jim Jermyn of Edrom Nurseries in Berwickshire for editing the translation. I hope that in this edition the book will reach thousands more readers.

Encounters with Blue Flowers

This book deals with gentians. There are of course gentians with yellow, white and red flowers, but this does not alter the fact that the predominant colour of this genus is blue.

World War II was not long over and one still could not travel very far. Innsbruck was the destination and a cable car carried us up to the Hafelekar. The path from the intermediate station led into a depression where the ground was fairly moist and had been heavily manured by grazing animals. Never since that day have I again seen trumpet gentians in such profusion and in such brilliant nuances of deep blue.

Even an autumn walk on the Bindlacher Berg, a hill near my home, left me, then a gardening beginner, amazed. *Gentianella aspera* ssp. *sturmiana* grew in clumps on the unploughed strips between the fields, its blue tint somewhat muted. Though only a biennial plant, to the as yet inexperienced youngster it seemed wonderful to find such beauty in the countryside so near home.

Late one summer a round trip took me through all the states which make up Yugoslavia. Starting from Macedonia, I crossed into Montenegro close to the northern point of Albania over the Čacor Pass. The plants at the roadside were covered in dust, yet even as I drove past gleams of blue caught my eye. My curiosity was aroused and closer inspection revealed the willow gentian, a type having a beautiful mid-blue tone in contrast to the duller, darker blues of the type found in the Alps.

It was mid-June; it had been a cool spring and the drive over the Furka Pass was still rather difficult. The snow plough had cleared only the outer half of the mountain road and on the descent we were glad to find stretches where we could again use the full breadth of the roadway. We halted by an alpine meadow covered with scattered remnants of melting snow and seamed with countless rivulets. Flowering there were birdseye primroses and spring gentians, *Primula farinosa* and *Gentiana verna*, both presenting nuances of colour which are seen only under the intense light of high altitudes with its increased ultraviolet component.

We were on Mount Elbrus in the central Caucasus, on 20 July. The two volcanic domes of this mountain—over 5,000m (16,000 ft) high—were covered with snow, as were the huge mountains around us. The contrast between the cloudless, brilliant blue sky and the snow-covered peaks never fails to fascinate the traveller, to whatever part of the world his journey might take him. Below 3,000m (9,600 ft) the mountains were free from snow and the dark rocks were visible, partly lava scree, partly obsidian in brown and black, adorned with beautiful lichens.

The intense light and the dark background gave the alpine plants a fabulous luminosity, and even our photographs profited from it. *G. verna* var. *angulosa*, growing there in unexampled profusion, presented a splendid blue which was heightened by the contrast with plants of other colours growing among it, notably the pure yellow scurvy grass (*Draba rigida* var. *imbricata*) and the beautiful pink flower-heads of *Primula darialica*. Yet another note was struck by *G. pyrenaica* (syn. *G. djimilensis*). It was an extraordinary experience, here at the south-eastern boundary between Europe and Asia, to find a plant which in western Europe is confined to the Pyrenees. Its individual blossoms are larger than those of *G. verna* var. *angulosa*, but the blue is muted and tinged with red. As if this were not enough, on the same hillside we found a pale blue biennial species (*Gentianella* spec.), together with scattered plants of *G. septemfida* growing among yellow daphnes (*Daphne glomerata*) and dense cushions of house leek (*Sempervivum pumilum*).

A journey to Alaska and through the Canadian Yukon brought more encounters with gentians. Flowing through Alaska is the mighty Tanana river, flanked by numerous gravel banks in summer when most of the snowmelt water has subsided. Flowering on the raised banks was a pretty *Erigeron* with white aster-like flowers, attractive enough for any garden. Growing among it to roughly the same height of 40–50cm (15–19 in) were pretty, deep-blue gentians, *Gentianella barbata*. They made a peaceful picture in the warm midday sun, a pleasure spoilt only by aggressive mosquitoes.

In the Denali Park, dominated by the tallest peak of North America, Denali (formerly Mount McKinley) over 6,000m (19,600 ft) in altitude, there is a luxuriant alpine flora on the lower slopes at 1,100 to 1,300m (3,600–4,300 ft). Our genus is represented by *G. glauca*, perhaps not as impressive as the Alpine gentians, but a peculiar plant with closed, bottle-shaped flowers of a colour best described as steel blue.

In the Canadian Yukon our journey took us along one of the most northerly gravel roads of the continent, the Dempster Highway, through the Ogilvie mountains. Crossing a pass, we suddenly spotted small white clumps on the slopes on either side. Closer inspection showed that it was *G. algida*, the Arctic gentian, here growing to heights of up to 35cm (14 in), considerably taller than the dimensions given in the books.

In southern Alaska, where mountain goats and white Alaskan sheep gambolled on the steep slopes on either side of Cook Inlet, *Gentianella amarella* was growing among *Echinopanax* and red baneberry. This gentian relative, with its pale reddish-violet flowers, is widely distributed throughout the circumpolar regions.

To such remote and romantic corners of the globe I have been privileged to travel in search of the gentian species in the wild. However, for those of us who do not wander so far, these subjects can be successfully cultivated at home—a source of constant delight.

Popular Concepts and Garden History

Most people have heard of gentians, even though they have not much interest in nature or gardening. Gentians and edelweiss are symbols of the alpine flora and indeed of the alpine world itself, and hence figure widely in arts and crafts, fashion and advertising; one example is the misleading illustration on the label of a brand of gentian *schnaps* (Figure 1). In the ordinary citizen's mind the word 'gentian' calls up an image of the trumpet gentian, in other words a *Gentiana acaulis* type. Yet the genus *Gentiana* offers such a wealth of species that even the expert sometimes finds something to surprise him.

It is not even possible to say how many species the genus comprises. Figures given in the literature range from 200 to 600 species, and there are some authors who suggest that the number may be even higher. One reason for this is that botany is not a dead science but very much alive (for those whose concern is purely horticultural it is sometimes a bit *too* lively). The status of a taxon in the hierarchy of botanical systematics may change as research progresses, for example a species in the botanical sense may become a subspecies or vice versa. Similar changes may be imposed at other levels, and *Gentiana* has even been split into several genera. In the past the correct figure may have been around 400 species at a time when the genus *Gentiana*, though subdivided into the subgenera *Eugentiana* Kusnezow and *Gentianella* Kusnezow, was still united.

Recently, however, the subgenus *Gentianella* has been granted the status of a genus. The morphological features which distinguish it are not very striking; everything centres on the membranous folds or plicae connecting the corolla segments, which are present in *Gentiana* but absent in *Gentianella*. This leaves roughly 200 species in the genus *Gentiana*. Furthermore, even today new species of gentian are still being discovered, a fact which accounts for some of the discrepancies in the roll call of the genus as cited in the literature.

As might be expected, a genus with so many members is not restricted to a narrow range but represented throughout the world. The cradle of the genus may perhaps be in Asia, and in geological terms the genus has been present since the Tertiary period, though after the end of the last Ice Age its spread seems to have come to a halt. Despite their wide distribution gentians have only feeble powers of migration; for example, some 92 per cent of the Asiatic species are restricted to that continent.

Gentiana algida is an exception which has migrated to North America. The only species which have migrated over wide areas are *Gentiana acaulis*, the trumpet gentian, and *G. verna*, the spring gentian. The latter is found not only in the Alps, but also in Siberia, in the Caucasus and even in North America. Although the main centre of the genus lies in Asia, the centre of the sub-genus *Gentianella* is located in South America with outliers extending to Malaysia and Australia. In this instance migration continued in the post-glacial period.

The main areas of distribution are to be found in the mountains of the northern temperate zone and the Andes in South America. In the lowlands there are relatively few species, and in the Arctic the genus is poorly represented. Their abilities as mountain climbers are shown by the fact that gentian species have been found on Mount Everest at altitudes as high as 5,500m (18,000 ft).

Most species of gentian have blue flowers, but there are some with white, yellow, red and even green flowers. Having nectaries situated deep within the flower, they are in general adapted to pollination by bumblebees and butterflies. One exception is the yellow gentian, *G. lutea*, which makes its nectar easily accessible to almost all insects, as testified by its good seedset under garden conditions.

Most species of gentian are perennial, only a small number being annual or biennial. Some are erect and others form mats. The leaves are opposite and usually sessile, less frequently single or confined to the base, where they are joined into a sheath encircling the stem. The flowers are radially symmetrical (actinomorphic), large and conspicuous in most species and usually carried in cymes. The number of stamens is the same as the number of corolla segments. The ovary is single chambered and contains numerous ovules. The seed is numerous and very fine, winged in some species and unwinged in others.

Because of their splendid flowers and also for the sake of the bitter substances present in the roots, some species of gentian have been mercilessly exploited by man. For this reason gentians are now protected in most countries, notably in central Europe. There is no reason to regret this. We can admire the wild species in their natural state without needing to take them home. Some of the finest species suitable for general garden cultivation are widely offered by nurseries, while others with more exacting requirements are obtainable from specialist alpine plant nurseries; given a little effort, almost every species can be found.

Gentians were known in antiquity though they did not have the same prominence as roses, iris, lilies or primulas. Dioscorides and Pliny tell us that King Gentius of Illyria caused a remedy against plague to be prepared from the leaves and roots. According to legend it was Hermes who showed the king the plant. The plant was then named in honour of Gentius and this name was later applied to the entire genus.

G. lutea, the yellow gentian, is referred to in the *Capitulare de Villis* of Charlemagne. Walafrid Strabo, Abbot of Reichenau in the ninth century, may well have known some species of gentian although he did not describe any in detail. Clusius added the trumpet gentian to the species already known in his time. Its brilliant blue must have inspired some monastic gardener to take this plant under his protection. One or two species of gentian are depicted in early still-life paintings, for example in 1730 by Robert Furbus in 'Twelve Months of Flowers', in which *G. acaulis* is unmistakably recognisable in the pictures for September and December; there is of course no connection between the months named and the flowering time. P. J. Redouté's picture of *G. acaulis* with a butterfly is doubtless known to many readers.

Gentians are also referred to in early herbals; for example, in the *Kreutterbuch* of Dioscorides dating from 1610 the 'Gross Entian' and 'Klein Entian' are illustrated and described. The 'Gross Entian' is undoubtedly *G. lutea*, but the 'Klein Entian' is not so easily identified and appears to be *G. cruciata*.

The nineteenth century saw gardeners taking an increasing interest in gentians. In the floral lexicon by H. Jäger, *Die schönsten Pflanzen des Blumen- und Landschaftsgartens, der Gewächshäuser und Wohnungen* (1873) no fewer than 21 species are listed. The creation of natural alpine gardens within botanical gardens demonstrated the breadth and variety of the genus to a wider public, and led to the construction of numerous private rock gardens. In 1903 *Möller's Deutsche Gärtner-Zeitung* listed as many as 68 species. Interest received a further stimulus from the discovery of the Chinese autumn-flowering species by British plant-hunters. Their introduction made it possible for gardeners to have gentians in flower continuously from early spring to late autumn. Furthermore, these new species brought completely novel shades of blue into the garden, some such as pure ultramarine blue and turquoise —almost unknown in any other flower.

In the present century gardeners have shown growing interest in gentians. In his first book *Winterharte Blütenstauden und Sträucher der Neuzeit* (Hardy Perennials and Shrubs for the Modern Garden) (1911), Karl Foerster mentioned only four species of gentian, *G. acaulis*, *G. asclepiadea*, *G. lutea* and *G. septemfida*. In *Der Steingarten der sieben Jahreszeiten* (The Rock Garden of the Seven Seasons) published just after World War II, their number had grown to 16. The well-known German garden writer Wilhelm Schacht did much to popularise gentians, most notably in the numerous editions of his book on rock gardening. Professor Richard Hansen, for many years Director of the Plant Trials Garden at Weihenstephan, did a great deal in his publications to disseminate information on gentians and tips for their use. An enormous range of species and varieties is nowadays available from specialist alpine nurseries. Even at the end of the nineteenth century, Sündermann at Lindau offered an impressive selection, while a new catalogue from Eschmann at Emmen in Switzerland contains 140 species and varieties. There are no limits to the opportunities now open to the gentian enthusiast.

Gentians through the Seasons

Gentians in spring and early summer—from sky-blue to ultramarine

The dream of every gardener is a broad luxuriant carpet of brilliant-blue spring gentians, accompanied by a clump of the native lady's slipper orchid (*Cypripedium calceolus*) or the prophet flower (*Arnebia pulchra*, syn. *A. echioides*). There can be hardly any other alpine which is more often bought and planted—and yet how often does it become permanently established? Our spring gentians are simply not like aubretias or cushion phloxes; despite some degree of hybridisation in certain garden forms, they are still wild plants with the characteristics of a true species. Any routine system of cultivation in which all plants are treated alike will certainly lead to failure.

The plants known as spring gentians have as their only common feature brilliant-blue flowers in every shade, opening in the spring. In other respects they are a medley of different forms and types with differing needs. These differences in requirement in such matters as position, soil moisture, drainage and soil reaction are one reason why these brilliant-blue alpines have never been successfully raised in our gardens.

Spring-flowering gentians can be divided into two groups, the *acaulis* group and the *verna* group. These names are derived from their two main representatives, *G. acaulis* (the trumpet gentian) and *G. verna* (the spring gentian). But matters now become more complicated. *G. acaulis* is a well-known name used by Linnaeus in 1753, though exactly what plant he intended to describe is not entirely clear. It might be either the lime-hating species *G. kochiana* or the 'limestone trumpet gentian' *G. clusii*. These two names have long been used by botanists, and the name *G. acaulis* was until recently regarded as a useful overall designation which also comprised the garden hybrids derived from the group. Recent research, however, has resolved the issue, and *G. acaulis* is now the valid name and should be used in place of *G. kochiana*. The new *Flora Europaea* lists seven species belonging to the acaulis group: *G. acaulis* L. (syn. *G. kochiana* Perr. et Song.), *G. alpina* Vill., *G. angustifolia* Vill., *G. clusii* Perr. et Song., *G. dinarica* Beck., *G. ligustica* R. de Vilmorin et Chopinet and *G. occidentalis* Jakowatz.

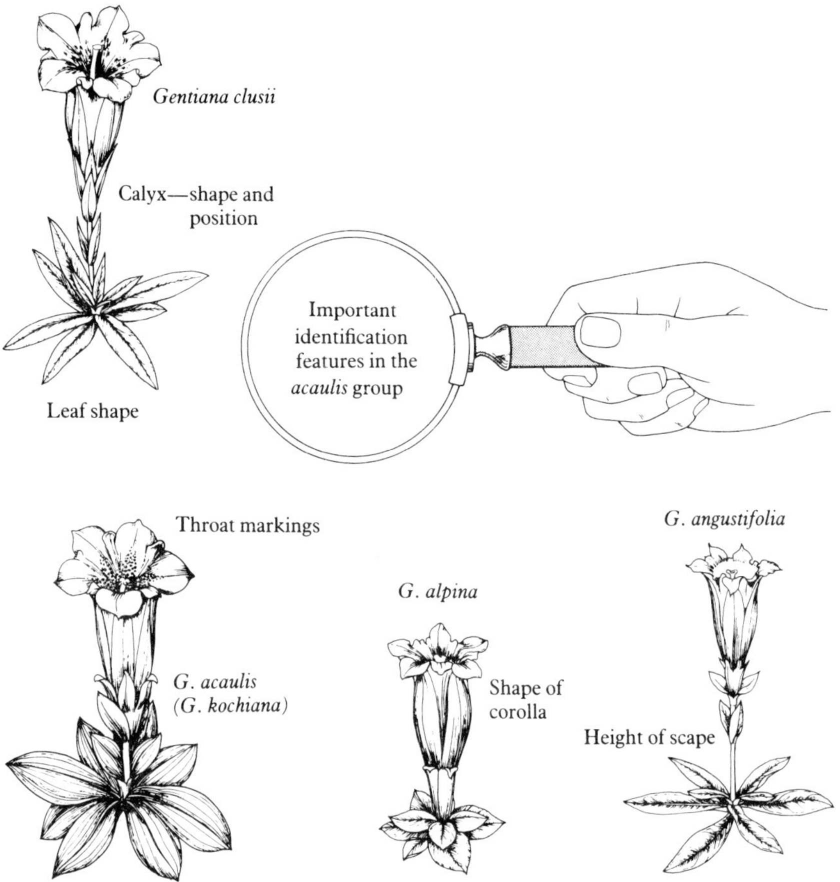

Figure 1 Important identification features in the acaulis *group*

Not all the species mentioned are worthy of a place in the garden, and even those which are suitable vary greatly in their soil requirements, lime tolerance or intolerance being a major factor. Details will be found under the descriptions of species, but a few hints can be given here. *G. acaulis* (syn. *G. kochiana*) is only just lime tolerant, *G. alpina* is lime hating, *G. angustifolia* is lime loving, while *G. clusii* and *G. dinarica* both require lime. Between all these species there are garden hybrids whose origins are not always entirely certain. In general these hybrids are more tolerant of variations in soil reaction than are the wild species. Most of the hybrids are lime tolerant, probably because *G. alpina*, a plant of acid soils, plays little or no part in their ancestry.

As for the physical properties of the soil, no clear recommendations can be made. For example, experiments in the trials garden at Weihenstephan produced results at variance with experience gained in many years' cultivation in my own garden. The best results are given by soils which consist of loam and sand mixed with humus and limestone chippings. The soil should be cool and moisture retentive, and should not warm up too rapidly. For this reason south-facing sites in full sun are unsuitable while west-facing positions are good. When grown in the same places the hybrids and selected forms often differ in vigour of growth, mat formation and freedom of flowering, but these discrepancies are no doubt attributable to their differences in parentage.

G. angustifolia and its hybrids seem to find lighter soils more to their liking than do the other species. One often hears that manuring is unnecessary, but my personal experience contradicts this. When flowering slackens, the plants will be grateful for a sprinkling of hoof and horn, bonemeal or even well-rotted pulverised cow manure (Cofuna, Californian cow dung), but moderation must always be the watchword.

G. dinarica is perhaps the best of the species for the beginner, while the best of the hybrids is *G.* 'Angustifolia hybrids Frei' with its huge trumpets on strong stalks; equally suitable is the *G. angustifolia* hybrid 'Holzmann', which often has a second flowering in autumn. Somewhat less vigorous is *G.* 'Gedanensis' with its ultramarine flowers. Other garden-worthy types are mentioned under the species descriptions.

What are the best places for planting trumpet gentians? Sites in the rock garden or alpine garden are certainly most appropriate, though the term rock garden need not be interpreted too strictly; a raised bed or a narrow strip beside the house may be equally suitable. Troughs and movable plant containers are just as good, provided they are placed where they do not get too hot (a lining of Polystyrene slabs will help to prevent this). Spots shaded by dwarf shrubs, evergreen or deciduous, are useful for gentians and other alpines with similar requirements.

There are plenty of suitable associates. Gentians and edelweiss are often spoken of together, and rightly so, for the edelweiss, contrary to popular belief, prefers moisture-retentive soil. A gardener seeking to simulate nature would combine it with *Carex firma*, tussock sedge, and *Sesleria albicans*, moorgrass. However, most gardeners desire a decorative effect and choose the background accordingly. The lady's slipper orchid (*Cypripedium calceolus*) and the prophet flower (*Arnebia pulchra*, syn. *A. echioides*) have already been mentioned. Blue and yellow always make attractive combinations. The yellow alpine auricula makes a good partner for trumpet gentians, while quieter tones can be provided by small ladies' mantles (*Alchemilla hoppeana*). There are plenty of rock-garden plants which flower at this season, but it is best to avoid unduly vigorous species which might soon overwhelm the clump of gentians.

The second group of spring-flowering gentian species, subspecies, varieties and forms is centred around *G. verna*, the spring gentian, and they are sometimes spoken of as the *verna* group. These gentians are a good deal more delicate than the trumpet gentians, their blue tints are brighter and they often display a brilliant sky-blue. They are less frequently seen in cultivation and are more difficult to keep. Although the spring gentian growing in thin turf over limestone and on rock ledges so often delights the rambler in the Alps, attempts to transplant it to the garden nearly always fail, even if it is dug up with a large root-ball. *G. verna* seems to depend to some degree on association with a root fungus. Its habitat in the limestone Alps demonstrates its tolerance of lime, but in the garden it seems to prefer a moorland soil consisting of sandy loam with peat. Sphagnum (peat moss) in finely divided form is evidently beneficial. The situation should be sunny but not too hot; here again, planting in shallow depressions is advantageous.

G. verna has a number of close relatives throughout the Alps. Of these only the Triglav gentian is somewhat more amenable to garden culture, but it is extremely tiny, being only 3 to 5cm (1¹⁄16 to 2 in) tall, and forming small mats of low shoots closely covered with overlapping leaves. It is lime tolerant, as is the karst gentian, *G. tergestina*, which begins to flower later but grows somewhat taller. The latter is not restricted to the karst districts, but extends from the southern Alps as far as the southern Carpathians. More difficult in culture are the round-leaved gentian, *G. orbicularis*, only 2 to 5cm (¾ to 2 in) tall, and *G. bavarica*, the Bavarian gentian, which can grow up to 20cm (8 in).

Here again there are nomenclatural difficulties. There is a variety of *G. verna* of frequent occurrence in the mountains of Asia, from Siberia to Mongolia and also in the Caucasus. It is commonly known by the name *G. verna* var. *angulosa*, though sometimes simply as *G. angulosa*. The author has found this form in the Caucasus growing on pure volcanic rubble without any limestone. Elsewhere there is a yellow-flowered type which goes under the name *G. verna* var. *oschtenica* (syn. *G. oschtenica*). *G. verna* var. *angulosa* is a much easier garden plant than *G. verna* from the Alps; it is sometimes offered in specialist plant catalogues and is quite commonly seen in British nurseries. The gardener who wants to grow these dainty spring gentians in the right surroundings will find appropriate models in nature. In the Alps *G. verna* is commonly accompanied by *Primula farinosa*, and in the Caucasus *G. angulosa* has *P. darialica* as its companion. Other companion plants are small sedges (*Carex firma*) and slow-growing androsaces. Such treasures

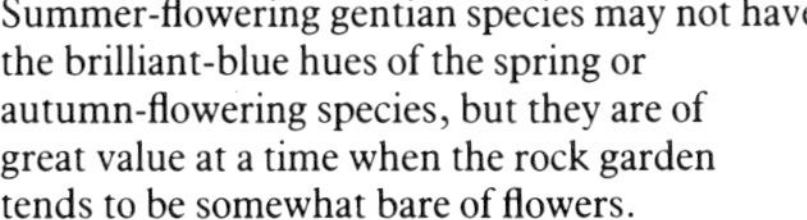

Summer-flowering gentian species may not have the brilliant-blue hues of the spring or autumn-flowering species, but they are of great value at a time when the rock garden tends to be somewhat bare of flowers.

Gentiana septemfida

Figure 2 Summer-flowering gentians

require choicer spots than the various trumpet gentians; they must be protected from invasive neighbours and from tall plants which might shade them out.

Especially in springtime, the lover of nature rejoices over each flower, for blue tints from sky-blue to ultramarine are uncommon in our gardens. The gardener will therefore make every effort to cultivate the various species, forms and hybrids of the spring gentian and to grow fine specimens. There are plenty of specialist nurseries where plant material is raised by experts (see under Suppliers). It should be a matter of honour for every plant-lover and gardener to leave undisturbed the gentians which grow in the wild.

Quiet blues in summer

The problem with the summer-flowering gentians is not so much nomenclatural difficulties as confusion of identity. The principal summer-flowering species available from nurseries are for the most part correctly named, but many of the less common species in cultivation are incorrectly identified. This applies both to plants and seeds.

Summer-flowering gentians are available in considerable numbers, and most of them are taller than the spring-flowering species. Their flowers are generally somewhat duller and less brilliant than those of the spring-flowering species. Most of them are suitable for growing in the rock garden. In view of the paucity of summer-flowering rock garden plants this is an advantage. All too often there is nothing to follow the gorgeous display of spring-flowering alpines. Although the splendours of spring cannot last right through to autumn, there is no reason why the gardener should not make full use of the available resources. Among these are the summer-flowering gentians, even though their blues are somewhat muted and they lack the clarity of line and form of the spring gentians.

One of the chief summer-flowering species is *G. septemfida*, offered by many nurseries. There are several varieties, notably *G. septemfida* var. *lagodechiana* and *G. septemfida* 'Doeringiana', both of them relatively undemanding plants and able to stand sunny conditions and even some degree of dryness at the roots. *G. septemfida* flourishes in soil between pH 6 and 7.5, although it is a native of Mount Elbus where it grows in pure lava grit with very little humus and a strongly acid reaction.

Another widely grown species is the cross gentian, *G. cruciata*. In the wild it favours open situations on dry limestone turf, its dark-blue flowers, greenish outside, opening in late summer (July–August). Being tolerant of dry conditions it makes a good plant for the rock garden and even for the heather bed, where it can be grown in association with such plants as sheep's fescue (*Festuca* species), dwarf inula (*Inula ensifolia* 'Compacta'), stemless thistle (*Carlina acaulis*), the Carthusian pink (*Dianthus carthusianorum*), now available in a more compact form, and the sulphur-yellow Balkan pink (*D. knappii*). There can be no objection to growing the cross gentian side by side with summer-flowering heaths (*Calluna* varieties), now available in many tints.

All the summer-flowering gentians mentioned so far are widely available and easily cultivated. A much more difficult plant is the marsh gentian (*G. pneumonanthe*), which has deep-blue flowers. From July to September it is to be seen in wet heaths on acid soil, but it will not succeed in the garden unless a suitable place is specially prepared for it. It varies considerably in height, some forms being as low as 10cm (4 in) and others as tall as 50cm (20 in). It is a plant for the specialist, who will grow the marsh gentian in a wet peat-bed along with such species as grass of Parnassus (*Parnassia palustris*), purple moorgrass (*Molinia caerulea*), and marsh gladiolus (*Gladiolus palustris*).

The less widely distributed species of summer-flowering gentians have deliberately not been considered in detail. However, those previously unacquainted with them will be surprised to find what a great variety of plants they can offer; their quiet blue tints and inconspicuous outlines are great assets to the rock garden, heather bed and wild garden in summer. On the other hand it must be said that many of the species are very much alike, in particular the relatives of the cross gentian (section Aperta).

Gentiana lutea, the perennial yellow gentian, from whose roots gentian schnaps is made (see p. 25), flowers in summer (June–August), and for various reasons deserves to be dealt with separately. This plant of the European mountains is not always easy to accommodate in the garden. In nature it grows on montane meadows, screes and alpine pastures up to altitudes of 2,500m (8,500 ft), and the rock garden is obviously a suitable place to grow it. The yellow gentian is one of those plants which is suited to supply variety. A sense of movement or contrast can be conveyed not only by the three-dimensional structure of the rock garden, but also by using plants of different heights. *G. lutea* grows to heights of between 50cm and 1.5m (20 in and 5 ft), and is one of the taller plants suitable for these special positions. Like the cross gentian it can also be used in heather beds and similar parts of the garden, especially as it prefers a sunny situation or light shade. However, it will not grow well in sandy soil which tends to dry out in summer; it requires moderately moist soil, somewhat loamy in composition. Most gardens have an area of wild planting where *G. lutea* can be fitted in. In any event a solitary position is preferable.

Although this gentian is an attractive wild perennial it is very seldom seen in gardens. This cannot be due to any difficulty in obtaining it; there are plenty of general and alpine nurseries which offer young plants. The main obstacle is the long time which the young plant requires to reach imposing dimensions—at least 4 to 6 years. During this time many young plants are eaten by slugs, overwhelmed by fast-growing neighbours or dug up by their disappointed owner because they take so long to flower. But patience will be repaid. The older one gets, the more one comes to value long-lived perennials whose age can be counted in decades. *G. lutea* can flourish on the same site for up to 60 years.

The yellow gentian is a good plant for a herb garden planned for a long-term future. It has a number of relatives, such as *G. burseri*, *G. pannonica*, *G. punctata* and *G. purpurea*, but they are less frequently seen in gardens. All of them are summer flowering and considerably smaller than our yellow gentian.

The willow gentian and its companions

G. asclepiadea is a tall-growing gentian widely distributed throughout central and southern Europe. Though a lime lover, it will grow well on mildly acid soils, and its late flowering season (August–September) makes the willow gentian a welcome garden plant. It is found in many of the mountain ranges of southern and central Europe up to altitudes of 2,200m (7,000 ft), usually in moist spots with loamy soil. In the garden it is best grown on the alpine or rock garden, in the peat bed, at the edge of a shrubbery or in the wild garden. The moister the soil, the more exposure to sun it will tolerate.

This wild perennial with attractively drooping stems 30 to 60cm (9 to 18 in) tall carries its flowers in clusters in the upper leaf axils, the leaves being arranged crosswise. *G. asclepiadea*, though not producing a blaze of colour, is a quietly attractive wild plant. Its flowers do not open until 8 or 9 o'clock in the morning, and by 5 or 6 o'clock at night they are closed again. The flower is dark sky-blue with reddish-violet dots in the interior. There is also a pretty albino form; recent selections include one with pink flowers and another which is light-blue and white. Unfortunately, even though all three colour types can be planted side by side, their flowering times hardly ever coincide. Then there are two local forms, *G. asclepiadea* 'Weisser Brunnen' (White Wells) from the Carpathians, with a pale throat, and 'Type Čakor' with mid-blue flowers, derived from the Čakor Pass in Montenegro on its southern border with Albania.

In nature the willow gentian is associated with ferns, white sneezewort, yellow monkshood and goatsbeard. A similar community can be created in the garden. However, there are other species suitable for the purpose, even though their flowering times are not always the same, such as *Astrantia carniolica* (masterwort), *Doronicum austriacum* (leopardsbane), *Geranium sylvaticum* (wood cranesbill), *Lilium martagon* (Turkscap lily), *Thalictrum aquilegifolium* (great meadowrue) and *Trollius* (globe flower) species. All of these prefer moist soil. Such tall plants naturally require a fairly large rock garden. If grown in light shade they need somewhat less moisture. If conditions are too dry for the willow gentian, its limp leaves soon show its distress. Such a pretty, late-flowering plant can also be grown to advantage among various sedges such as *Carex ornithopoda* 'Variegata' (birdsfoot sedge). *C. morrowii* 'Variegata' (variegated Japanese sedge), *C. plantaginea* (broad-leaved sedge), *C. siderostica* (hart's-tongue sedge), either in the plain green form or the variegated form, and the new dwarf introduction from

Japan, *C. conica* 'Hime-Kan-suge'. Some of the low-growing and less vigorous hostas also make suitable partners, and the late-flowering varieties can produce pleasing colour harmonies.

The willow gentian is an easily cultivated perennial which makes attractive clumps when well established. It offers great potential for growing in conjunction with other plants, and should not be neglected.

Autumn flowering gentians from China

The species of gentian discussed so far have been established in our gardens for many decades, unlike certain newcomers which were quite unknown in the nineteenth century. At the beginning of the twentieth century British plant hunters brought back these treasures from China, India, Burma and Tibet. *G. farreri* was first found in 1914 by Farrer and Purdom in Kansu on the northern border of the Himalayas, growing on high-altitude mountain pastures, and named after its discoverer. *G. sino ornata*, the most important species of autumn-flowering gentians, was discovered independently by several plant hunters: first in 1904 by George Forrest in north-western Yunnan and in 1910 in the Lichiang mountains, and later by Kingdon Ward further to the south-east. It flowered for the first time in Europe in 1912 in the Edinburgh Botanic Gardens, and only six years later the plants had spread into enormous carpets. Professor Balfour described the Chinese autumn-flowering gentian, *G. sino ornata*, as 'the finest and most valuable garden plant which has so far been introduced this century.' *G. veitchiorum* was discovered in Szechuan by the plant-hunting expedition sent out between 1904 and 1907 by the then world-famous firm of Veitch & Sons, Chelsea. In subsequent years it was followed by various other species which are now included in Section Frigidae.

Though in other sections it is the species rather than the varieties which have achieved prominence, here the opposite is the case. Although *G. farreri* and *G. sino ornata* are thriving species and worth growing in their own right, the autumn-flowering gentians as a whole are best known for the enormous variety of superb hybrids which they have produced.

Soon after the species had been introduced into cultivation came the first successful attempts at hybridisation. The first cross was *G. sino ornata* with *G. farreri*, and the outcome was *G.* × *macaulayi*, together with *G.* × *macaulayi* 'Wells Variety' (in the older literature sometimes given as *G.* × *macaulayi* var. *wellsii*). These hybrids are superior in certain respects to their parents, excellent as the latter are. They are splendid plants which grow vigorously and bear flowers in enormous profusion. The colour is a pure deep-blue, deeper than that of *G. farreri*. The flowers are larger and have divergent corolla lobes, so that flowering carpets of these hybrids are particularly colourful. Another important hybrid is *G.* × *stevenagensis* (*G. sino ornata* × *G. veitchiorum*). The pollen parent is somewhat stiff in its habit of growth and not very free flowering. The hybrid does not have these defects: its growth is laxer, and its flowers are larger and more profuse. *G.* × *hexa-farreri* (*G. farreri* × *G. hexaphylla*) is also of some value, though outshone by its gorgeous offspring, *G.* × *wealdensis* and *G.* 'Inez Weeks'. Among other hybrids are *G.* × *faroma* (*G. farreri* × *G. sino ornata*), *G.* 'Devonhall', *G.* 'Inverleith', *G.* × *vorna*, *G.* × *veora*, *G.* × *fasta* and *G.* × *orva*. Eschmann's alpine nursery (Emmen, Switzerland) lists some 60 different hybrids in this section. Many of these named varieties are of uncertain parentage, but this does not matter. The important point is that they represent a huge range of low-growing perennials.

Where can these jewels of autumn be planted? They are vigorous plants and will flourish provided their needs are met. In general they require a cool spot, in sun, with adequate atmospheric humidity. The soil should be a sandy loam of slightly acid reaction, enriched by addition of coarse peat and properly drained. As ever, there are individual exceptions, and *G. farreri* is lime-tolerant. The hybrid *G.* × *macaulayi* can also be grown in limestone soils with generous addition of peat. As there are so many hybrids, experiments are always worthwhile. As a rule, the more *G. farreri* 'blood' a hybrid has inherited, the more lime-tolerant it will prove.

A statement often repeated in books is that *G. sino ornata* presents little difficulty in cultivation or in propagation. That is true, but only if the soil reaction is really acid. This is an absolute necessity. The following paragraph applies only to cultivation in lime-free districts.

When first planted out *G. sino ornata* should if possible be obtained as pot-grown plants. The chosen place should be bright, but certainly not exposed to burning sun; steep, south-facing slopes are totally unsuitable. Though well-established plants will withstand a certain degree of drought, adequate soil moisture must be ensured. A partially shaded spot shielded from direct sunshine is ideal, and if much exposure to the sun is unavoidable, then shallow depressions should be scooped out. This species will tolerate finely divided humus soil or peat. A certain proportion of black acid-peat is beneficial. The entire compost can be fairly rich, and well-rotted cow manure will encourage vigorous growth. The moister the atmosphere, the better *G. sino ornata* will flourish. A stream, a pond or even a waterlily pool nearby will have good effects. Where a garden does not provide adequate atmospheric humidity, assiduous watering will be needed in high summer. Yet if the water contains lime all these efforts will be in vain. Daily sprinkling is a duty at this time of year. A peat bed is the most reliable site, though a suitable spot may be found in the rock garden. Even a place at the edge of a heather garden may serve the purpose, provided it is not too hot.

At the other extreme is *G. farreri*, which, as already mentioned, is lime tolerant, or will at least put up with a mildly alkaline soil reaction. Its blue is pretty enough, even though it is not the genuine article. A brilliant, pale turquoise-blue is found in hardly any other garden plant, the nearest to it being the colour of the morning glory (*Pharbitis nil*, synonym *Ipomoea imperialis* Hort.). In August and September, when not much else is flowering in the rock garden, this gentian displays its sky-blue splendours. Externally the flowers are whitish with greenish longitudinal stripes. It will stand rather more shade than the other species and hybrids. The dark azure blue of *G. sino ornata* makes a pleasing colour contrast, and the other species and hybrids lie between these two extremes. Albino forms of most of the species are available.

There are not many plants flowering at the same time which go well with autumn gentians. They produce a better effect against a quiet setting than in company with multicoloured neighbours. Small clumps of dwarf sedges (*Carex* species) are appropriate, as are miniature ferns. As a background behind the gentians *Begonia grandis* var. *evansiana* (hardy if given protection in winter) may be tried, but its height (60cm (24 in)) must be borne in mind. It may be worth experimenting with autumn-flowering cyclamens (*Cyclaman cilicium*, *C. hederifolium*). Heathers (*Calluna* species) might also be used; in particular those varieties with yellowish coloration contrast well with the blue flowers of the Chinese gentians.

Gentians of other colours

Everyone knows that gentian blue is a special kind of blue, and most people not interested in gardening or botany think that all gentians are blue. Though that may be true of the vast majority, there are many gentians of other colours. First, there are the much sought after albino forms of *G. verna* and the trumpet gentians of the acaulis group. White-flowered forms turn up occasionally, perhaps once among tens of thousands of plants. The Asiatic species also throw up white variants

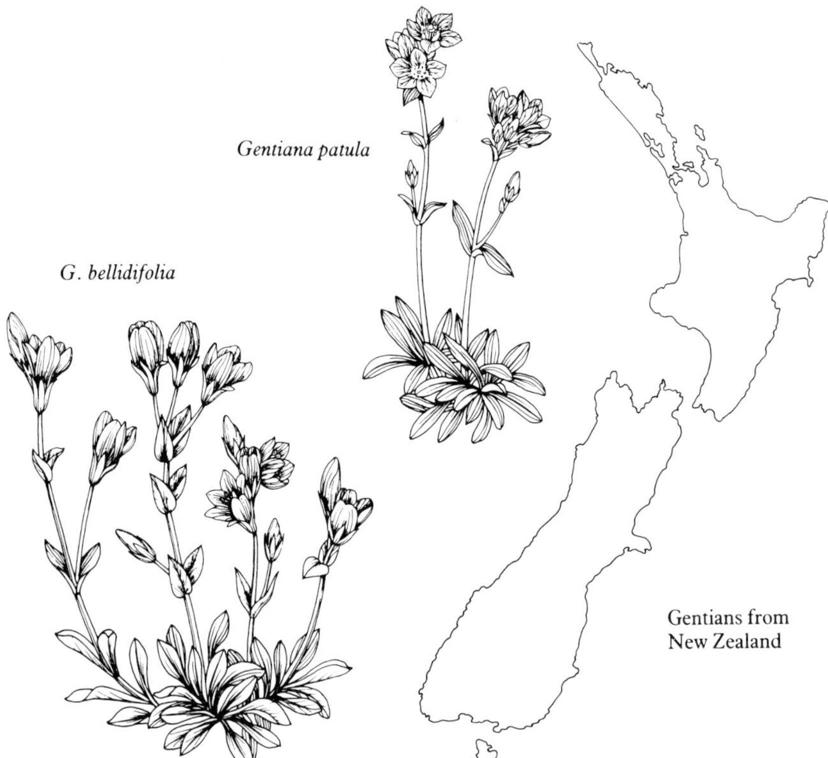

Figure 3 Gentians from New Zealand

from time to time. Some of these rarities are available from alpine nurseries, but supply is not always sufficient to meet demand. The tall European species are perhaps better known: *G. lutea* and *G. punctata* in shades of yellow and *G. purpurea* with reddish-purple flowers. The white and pink colour variants of the willow gentian have already been mentioned. In the Caucasus there is a rare yellow-flowered form of *G. verna* var. *angulosa* which goes under the name of *G. verna* var. *oschtenica* (syn. *G. oschtenica*). Another yellow-flowered species found in the Caucasus is *G. gelida*. There are also whitish and yellowish species among the Asiatic gentians (e.g. *G. tibetica*).

If we extend our survey to include *Gentianella*, nowadays a genus in its own right, we find an astonishing number of other colours. Although most of the European and Asiatic species of gentian have blue flowers, the South American species of *Gentianella* from the Andes display a bewitching palette of colours, chiefly gaudy reds and yellows, though white, pink, violet, brownish-purple and even greenish are also represented. Large numbers of them grow in Colombia, Venezuela, Ecuador, Peru and Bolivia. They are mountain flowers, often found at heights of 5,000m (16,400 ft) in the Andes. Unfortunately, none of them has yet become acclimatised to our conditions, and it seems doubtful whether any of these aloof and haughty South Americans will ever be at home in our gardens. At present most of them are known only from the fascinating accounts of travellers returning from those mountains.

Gentianella weberbaueri is a widely distributed species with red flowers. Its flowering time extends from May to June, depending on altitude. Yellow variants are occasionally found. The roots run very deep and the plants are almost impossible to extract. *G. scarlatinostriata* has also attracted much interest. It has a faint resemblance to *Campanula medium* (Canterbury bells) and produces numerous large, yellow flowers with red stripes. *G. buchtenii* also has red flowers, while *G. formosissima* and *G. jamesoni* tend more towards carmine and purple. *G. tiosphaera* is pure sulphur-yellow. Apparently none of these species is colour stable. Seedlings produce flowers of many colours, and also vary greatly in height. Many of these species are at first sight quite unrecognisable as gentians. *Gentianella violacea*, for example, looks like a heather, with panicles of tiny, bell-shaped flowers. Alas, all these exotic beauties are still unobtainable.

Gentians from New Zealand are much more easily obtainable, although from the morphological angle they have little in common with our familiar species. Most of them have white flowers, some tinged with pale violet. *Gentiana saxosa* is widely grown in Great Britain.

Gentians in herbal medicine

The curative action of extracts from dried gentian root has been known since antiquity; Dioscorides and Pliny mention the yellow gentian (*G. lutea*) in this connection. This classical bitter is still obtainable from pharmacists (Gentian Root B.P. and E.P.). The recommended procedure for making a cold extract is to add a teaspoonful of dried, powdered gentian root to a cupful of water and leave it overnight. Alternatively it can be gently heated. The active principle is also present in an alcoholic extract and this is the preparation generally employed.

The crude drug contains two glycosides, gentiopicrin and amarogentin, which are among the most intensely bitter substances known.

Amarogentin is clearly perceptible to the taste buds in dilutions as extreme as 1:50,000. One can well imagine how little is present in commercial gentian schnaps. The connoisseur who enjoys this drink cannot claim that it has any medicinal value, yet this is not to belittle its value as a flavouring agent. Dried gentian root is also an important ingredient of herbal liqueurs. In somewhat higher concentrations it is used in the manufacture of various aperitifs and medicines intended to stimulate the appetite.

Besides gentiopicrin and amarogentin, the roots contain certain peculiar sugars, notably gentianose and gentiobiose. Also present in the fresh roots is the yellow pigment gentisin together with some tannin. The healing value depends on the tonic effect on the stomach, an effect manifest throughout the entire digestive system; the active principles enhance appetite and stimulate gastric secretion. This speeds up the emptying of the stomach into the duodenum, and swiftly relieves gastric upsets; an added advantage is that the drug has no tendency to cause constipation. One well-known use of gentian is as a remedy for lack of energy and anaemia, for which purpose it is prescribed in combination

Plate 1

Above left: a good form of *Gentiana sino ornata*, the parent of more hybrids than any other species.

Above right: 'Azurhimmel', a vigorous and beautiful hybrid raised by Walter Löw, Weiden. It forms large mats and is easily cultivated.

Centre left: The cultivar 'Delft', selected by Hermann Fuchs, Hof, presents a colour combination reminiscent of Delft tiles. Even the best colour printing can scarcely convey the magic of the natural colours.

Centre right: 'Inverleith', a cross from *G. farreri* × *G. veitchiorum*, is an old and well-tried plant with large flowers. The blue is extremely deep.

Below left: 'Susan Jane', raised by Jack Drake, a brilliant, deep azure-blue with a white throat. A good grower with long, creeping shoots.

Below right: *G. sino ornata* 'Praecox'. There is some doubt whether this is a geographical variant of the species or whether it is of hybrid origin. It provides long-lasting cut flowers for miniature vases.

with iron complexes and other roborants. It is also of some value as a febrifuge and causes slight elevation of blood pressure, an effect probably attributable to gentiopicrin; it has also been used as a remedy for malaria. In large doses it may have a depressant action, but smaller doses have a stimulant action on the central nervous system.

Apart from the yellow gentian, the roots of certain other species are utilised, notably the easily cultivated willow gentian *G. asclepiadea*. However, even in old plants the roots are only 1cm (3⁄8 in) in diameter. Other sources of the crude drug are the purple gentian, *G. purpurea*, and the spotted gentian, *G. punctata*. The stemless gentian of the limestone Alps, *G. clusii*, is occasionally mentioned in this connection, but its roots are too thin for the purpose and the whole plant has to be collected and dried. Its main use is for the preparation of Schnaps.

Gentian schnaps

Some will have seen the label of the bottle of gentian schnaps on which is emblazoned the bright blue trumpet gentian (*G. acaulis* group). The

Plate 2

For the layman the trumpet gentian, apart from the edelweiss, is the archetypal alpine flower. The ordinary amateur gardener regards *Gentiana acaulis* as a single species. Only when he studies the plants in great detail does he realise that the collective name trumpet gentian (*G. acaulis*) embraces a wide range of species and varieties with minor but important morphological differences and differing requirements when grown in the garden. *Flora Europea* lists seven different species. Not all are of equal garden merit, but the gentian enthusiast will wish to try the difficult species as well as the easier ones.

Above: *G. dinarica* is one of the species which present few problems. It is a lime-loving plant which grows vigorously and flowers reliably.

Below: *G. ligustica* is another lime-loving species which comes from the Maritime Alps and Central Appenines. Although a good garden plant, this gentian is not very often seen in our gardens.

Figure 4 A misleading label!

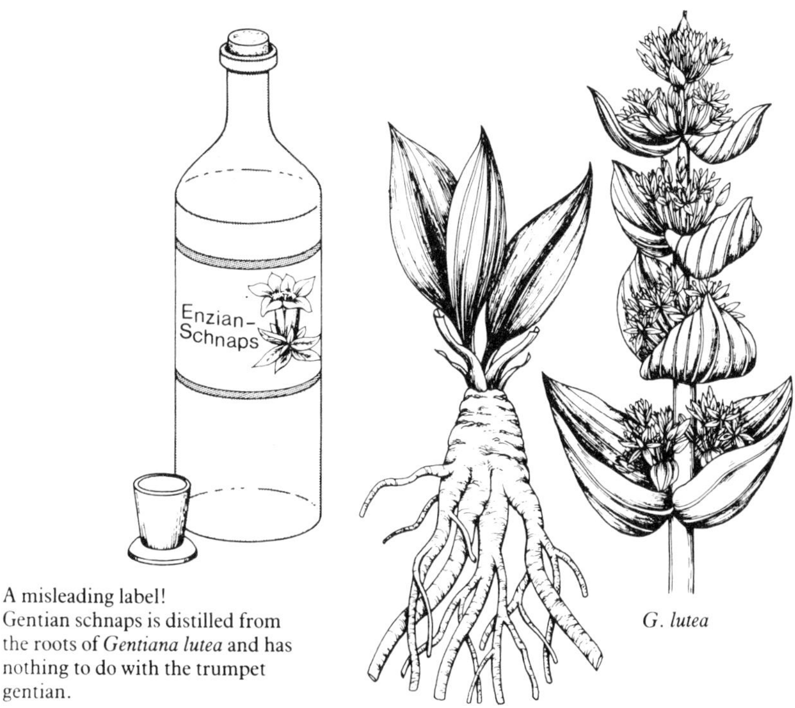

A misleading label!
Gentian schnaps is distilled from the roots of *Gentiana lutea* and has nothing to do with the trumpet gentian.

G. lutea

non-expert might be excused for thinking that this valuable stomachic is produced from that plant; but he would be astonished to learn that it is made from the roots of a tall perennial, *G. lutea*, the yellow gentian. To be an effective stomachic it does not need to be distilled.

Let me give you an example: the spring shoots put up by a five-year-old plant in my garden were destroyed by slugs. No further shoots appeared. The roots, then about as thick as a finger, were dug up and washed, cut into 5cm (2 in) lengths, split into pieces as thick as a pencil and dried. The material was then soaked in a litre of gin for several weeks and finally strained off. This concentrate was so strong that a tablespoonful added to a bottle of corn schnaps or gin gave a product many times stronger than commercial gentian schnaps. Such a homemade product may not be a pleasure to drink—the bitter, strongly earthy flavour may be far from enjoyable—but its effect on an upset stomach is surprisingly good.

In recent years efforts have been made to grow this medicinal plant on a field scale. The outcome seems to have been highly successful, and it is to be hoped that natural stocks will soon be spared further exploitation. At the International Garden Exhibition in Munich in 1983 an alpine meadow with a dense stand of *G. lutea* was one of the exhibits. Had it not been for all the garden plants around it, one might have thought oneself carried away to its natural habitat. Hundreds of visitors met the yellow gentian for the first time, and also the alcoholic beverage, which is both a schnaps and a medicine.

Growing Gentians

Gentians for the rock garden

Nearly all species of gentian are suitable for the rock garden. Nevertheless, they differ greatly in their requirements as regards position, soil type and soil reaction, and of course in their heights. Thought must also be given to the macroclimate and microclimate before attempting to grow certain difficult species.

Gentians are the main contributors of blue tints to the rock garden, yet considering the large numbers of rock gardens built by amateurs they are surprisingly seldom seen. Many gardeners start with trumpet gentians but soon give up in disappointment. Very often the soil is too light and insufficiently retentive of moisture and the chosen spot is too warm. If the plants are not garden hybrids but species or natural forms, they will require careful attention to soil reaction, attention which they do not always receive (see 'Gentians in spring and early summer'). To avoid disappointment the beginner should start with *Gentiana septemfida*, the most easily grown species, sometimes known as 'Everyman's Gentian'. Well-established plants grow into hemispherical bushes 15cm (6 in) high, which make a pleasing impression even though the flowers lack the true brilliance of gentian blue. The next to try is one of the trumpet gentians, not the tricky *G. acaulis* (syn. *G. kochiana*) but a vigorous species such as *G. dinarica* or *G. clusii*, or preferably one of the garden forms. The standard range for the ordinary rock-gardener might comprise the following species: *G. septemfida*, a species from the acaulis group, *G. asclepiadea*, *G. lutea* and *G. farreri* (or in gardens with acid soil *G. sino ornata* or one of its hybrids).

Any gardener who is really keen on gentians should take the first opportunity of reconstructing his or her rock garden so as to create a variety of suitable places for growing them. Best of all are spots in the shade cast by dwarf shrubs and large stones, and in depressions in the soil. The more varied the relief and contours of the rock garden, the more places it will offer for growing gentians, and the wider the range which will flourish. Special requirements can be met by mixing granite or limestone chippings with the soil. Measures to improve the soil are of special importance when autumn-flowering gentians are to be grown. Addition of peat and well-rotted cow manure, admixture of flowers of sulphur, watering with organic iron compounds such as chelated iron (Sequestrene), addition of small quantities of phosphoric acid to the water in the watering can—all these are measures which can be employed in limestone districts to create and maintain an acid soil reaction. Sometimes part of the rock garden is planned as a peat bed, with peat blocks in place of rocks. Only in such conditions will the marsh gentian (*G. pneumonanthe*) and the purple gentian (*G. purpurea*) feel at home. Many species of gentian will not flourish without high atmospheric humidity, and in regions with dry summers daily spraying is necessary. The best results are obtained with a built-in mist system, operated automatically by a time switch (see *Saxifrages*, Fritz Köhlein, Batsford, 1984).

Like all small perennials, gentians have a limited flowering time. Nevertheless, by choosing species with different flowering seasons the enthusiast can have gentians in flower from the end of April until the first frosts of autumn. The final display of the year is given by the autumn-flowering Asiatic gentians, supported by occasional late flowers from the spring-flowering trumpet gentians. Care must be taken to choose appropriate neighbours which flower at the same time and provide pleasing colour combinations. Suitable associations are *G. verna* and *Primula farinosa* (birdseye primrose), *G. acaulis* types and *Arnebia pulchra* (syn. *A. echioides*), *G. septemfida* and *Inula ensifolia* 'Compacta', *G. farreri* and *Sedum cauticolum*.

The gardener who is more adventurous and wants to grow some of the more exacting gentian species will have to look them up in the list of species and choose ones to meet his wishes. This often needs a shift to the 'natural' rock garden (the 'Alpinum'). Attractive appearance and easy cultivation are no longer the prime requisites. The aims now are plant groupings which are true to nature, association with other plants which are ecologically appropriate, or subdivision into geographical compartments—for example gentians from the Alps, gentians from the Caucasus, from Japan, from mainland Asia and from New Zealand.

Although it is true that nearly all species of gentian are suitable for the formal rock garden and the 'natural' rock garden, due regard must be paid to their stature. A giant such as *G. lutea* is out of place in a little rock garden, though it is entirely fitting in a rock garden planned on a grander scale.

Gentians in the alpine house

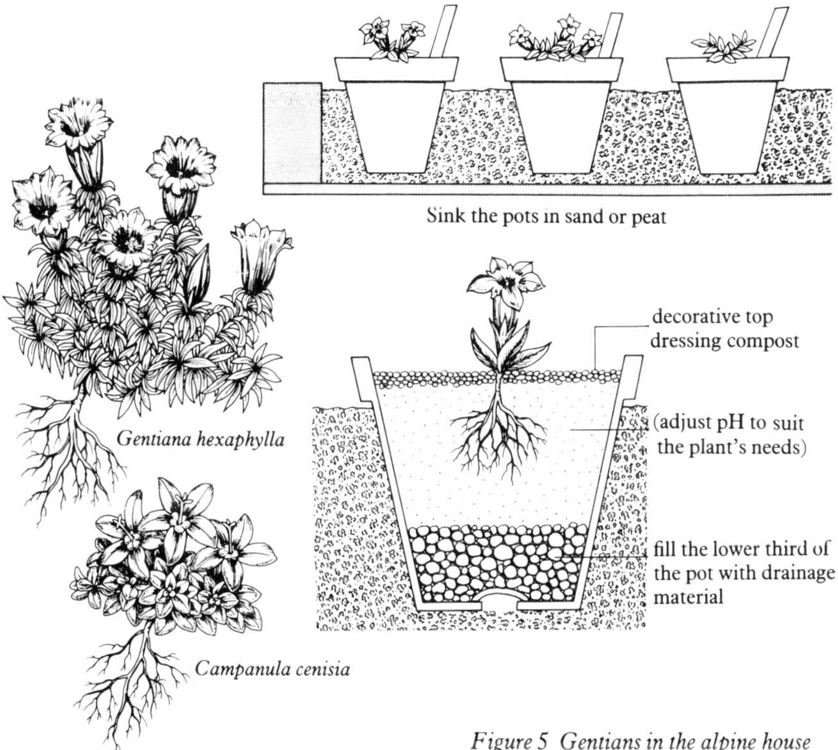

Figure 5 Gentians in the alpine house

Gentians for the alpine house

The alpine house is not the place to grow the familiar gentians discussed in the foregoing section. Nevertheless, the genus includes a considerable number of species which are suitable for alpine-house cultivation. The idea that any small greenhouse can be used for growing alpine plants—a notion encouraged by some greenhouse manufacturers—is not correct. An alpine house must be constructed so as to provide generous ventilation, so that the internal temperature in summer does not rise more than a few degrees above the temperature of the surrounding air. This can be achieved only by providing large ventilation spaces (removable side-panels and large roof-panels which can be opened widely). A thermostatically controlled ventilator is a valuable accessory. The cultivation of exacting species under alpine-house conditions has made great strides in Great Britain, but elsewhere the cult of the alpine house is only just beginning.

The species of gentian suitable for alpine-house cultivation are seldom planted out of doors at ground level or in raised beds, though in many cases that might be entirely feasible. They are best grown in medium-sized clay pots, partially or completely sunk in sand. This allows moisture to diffuse from the outside into the pot and vice versa. A generous layer of drainage material at the bottom of the pots is necessary even though the plants are protected from rain; without it they can too easily be killed by over-watering. Plants can be transferred between the alpine house and the cold frame. After the gentians have flowered they can be moved into the cold frame and left there exposed to the weather until late autumn, when they are once more brought back into the alpine house. The composition of the compost used to fill the pots needs even more care and thought than is necessary when making soil mixtures for outdoor planting.

Plants in pots are more trouble to water than plants in the open ground, but their water supply can be more easily controlled. A decorative top dressing is helpful in checking the growth of moss. Before choosing the top dressing, some thought must be given to its effects on the compost and the pH. Depending on the plant's requirements, there are various materials which can be used: pumice grit, ground lava, granite or marble chippings or any other locally available stone chippings. Species which enjoy boggy soil can be dressed with well-rotted cow manure, and use can even be made of sintered clay nodules—the material used for hydroponic culture—provided it is not too coarse (Hydroleca(R)).

Small amounts of manure are tolerated while the plants are not in flower, but caution is necessary. Liquid Peru guano may be added in small quantities to the contents of the watering can, but only for those species which prefer slightly alkaline or neutral soil. Gentians which demand acid conditions should be given a little Alkrisal solution instead. If in doubt, it is better to give too little fertiliser than too much.

A list of gentians for the alpine house will depend on individual tastes, but the emphasis will be on the smaller and less easily grown species. The following list makes no claim to completeness, but may offer a few ideas:

G. bavarica
G. brachyphylla
G. cachemirica
G. depressa
G. farreri
G. georgei
G. gilvostriata
G. × hexa-farreri
G. hexaphylla
G. imbricata
G. veitchiorum
G. lawrencei
G. loderi
G. × macaulayi
G. ornata
G. pyrenaica
G. saxosa
G. stragulata
G. verna var. oschtenica
G. acaulis
G. verna var. alba
G. acaulis var. alba
G. angustifolia
G. clusii
G. alpina
G. froelichii
G. 'Inverleith' (*G. farreri* × *G. veitchiorum*)
G. kurroo
G. newberryi
G. prolata

Propagation from seed

Propagation by seed is widespread for the species, though not for cultivars. It is particularly useful when plants are required in large numbers, and for rare species which are not available as living plants, though their seed may be obtainable from the seed exchanges and other sources.

Regrettably, seed is often sold to amateurs at the wrong time of year. Gentian seed needs cold for germination, and it is misleading to offer seed in packets with brightly coloured pictures of the trumpet gentian in April, May or later. Sowings at this season will produce hardly any seedlings. As with most plants, the fresher the seed, the higher the percentage of germination.

Gentian seed is fine, but not so fine as to be difficult to handle. Mixing with sand or other vehicles is not usually necessary. The amount of seed needed to produce 1,000 plants is about 5g (1/5 oz) for the larger species (*G. lutea*, *G. purpurea*, *G. punctata*, *G. tibetica*), 2g (1/10 oz) for *G. acaulis*, *G. angustifolia*, *G. clusii*, *G. dinarica*, and about 1g (1/20 oz) for *G. asclepiadea*, *G. brachyphylla*, *G. cruciata*, *G. dahurica*, *G. gracilipes*, *G. septemfida*. Species with extra fine seed include *G. nipponica*, *G. pneumonanthe*, *G. triflora* and *G. verna* and its relatives; about 0.5g (1/40 oz) seed will yield 1,000 plants.

Commercial nurserymen use seed boxes, but for amateurs clay pots or pans will suffice. Plastic pots should never be used, as they tend to hold stagnant moisture despite all attempts at ensuring drainage, and the compost soon becomes covered with moss. It is essential to prevent this as the seed pots often have to be left for long periods before germination

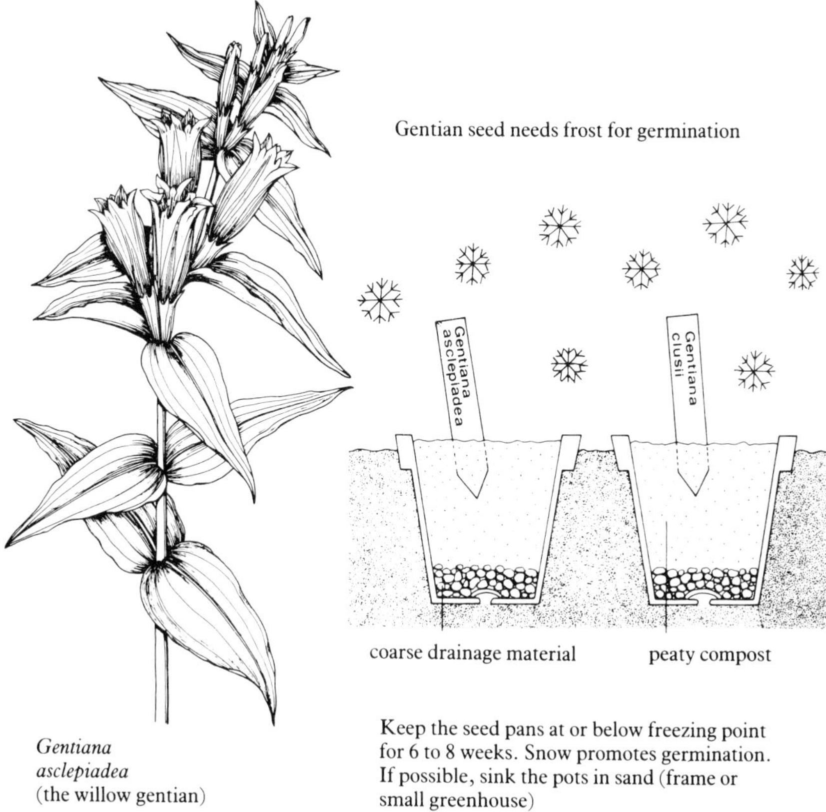

Figure 6 Gentians from seed

will occur. One useful tip is to cover the seed pots temporarily with dried chopped sphagnum moss, though this must be removed when spring comes. The more effectively the pots and compost are sterilised and the better the standards of hygiene in the seed frame, the less is the risk of moss growth. Seed pots placed in glasshouses or cold frames where there is an abundant growth of moss will swiftly be covered with a film of green. All pots must be thoroughly cleansed before use. The composition of the seed compost is not crucial, though it would obviously be a mistake to sow the seeds of species which require acid soil in a lime-containing compost. What is more important is to use a compost free from seeds, spores and bacteria. Commercial seed compost bought in plastic bags and mixed with an equal amount of sharp sand (river

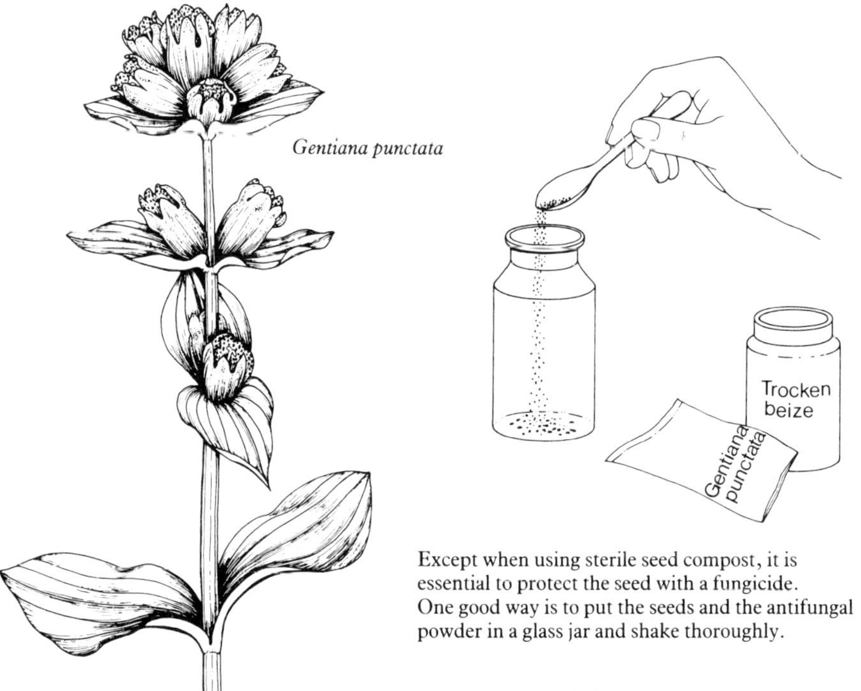

Except when using sterile seed compost, it is essential to protect the seed with a fungicide. One good way is to put the seeds and the antifungal powder in a glass jar and shake thoroughly.

Figure 7 Protecting the seed

sand, washed grit) gives good results. More attention must be given to the compost used for growing on the seedlings after they have been pricked out. After sprinkling the gentian seed on the surface of the compost it should be covered with the thinnest possible layer of compost sieved over it and gently pressed down. If the pots have to be watered from above, a watering can with a fine rose must be used; a coarse spray will wash the seeds to one side of the pan. It is important to remember that gentian seed needs darkness for germination; the pans must therefore be covered or placed in the dark.

As already mentioned, the earlier the seeds are sown, the better the yield. Seed harvested by the gardener can be sown in November or December, or even earlier. A period of at least 5–6 weeks at 0 to 5°C (32 to 41°F) is normally advisable for seeds which require cold for germination. Many alpines of this kind give good results when exposed to this temperature range. For gentian seed, however, it is better to expose the seed pans to slight frost, i.e. 0 to −5°C (32 to 23°F) for a longer period.

Repeated covering with snow is also advisable. It is advantageous to keep gentian seed pans at somewhat higher temperatures, say 10°C (50°F) for a few days after sowing, so as to give the seed time to absorb water and swell up, and then to start exposure to cold. In general, there are no great differences between species in the treatment which they require, though certain species do have special needs which are noted below.

G. affinis Likes a high proportion of peat in the seed compost. The seed pan should be kept in a shady spot. Best time for sowing: December–January.

G. altaica Likes a high proportion of fine grit in the compost, A strict calcifuge. January is the best time for sowing.

G. andrewsii Sow in January in ordinary compost.

G. asclepiadea Is unhappy if the seed pans are allowed to get too dry.

G. cachemirica Germination often poor: best results from fresh seed sown in August or September.

G. calycosa Sow in January, but does not require frost. Seed pans must not get too dry. Likes compost rich in humus, but not acid (a lime lover).

G. corymbifera Likes compost enriched with peat. Good results from fresh seed sown in September–October.

Gentianopsis crinita A short-lived species which requires periodic sowings. Sow in January in loamy compost. Pot up the seedlings early as they have brittle roots.

Gentiana georgei Sow in January in compost enriched with peat; a strict calcifuge. Do not let the pan get too dry.

G. gracilipes Sow in January in ordinary compost. Sowings in August–September will give even higher yields.

G. pneumonanthe Peat-rich compost, acid reaction. Keep seed pans moist.

G. prolata Although fully lime tolerant, it needs a high proportion of humus (leaf mould, peat).

G. saponaria Requires a high proportion of peat in the compost. Keep the seed pans moist.

G. saxosa Not very long lived, requires periodic sowings in January.

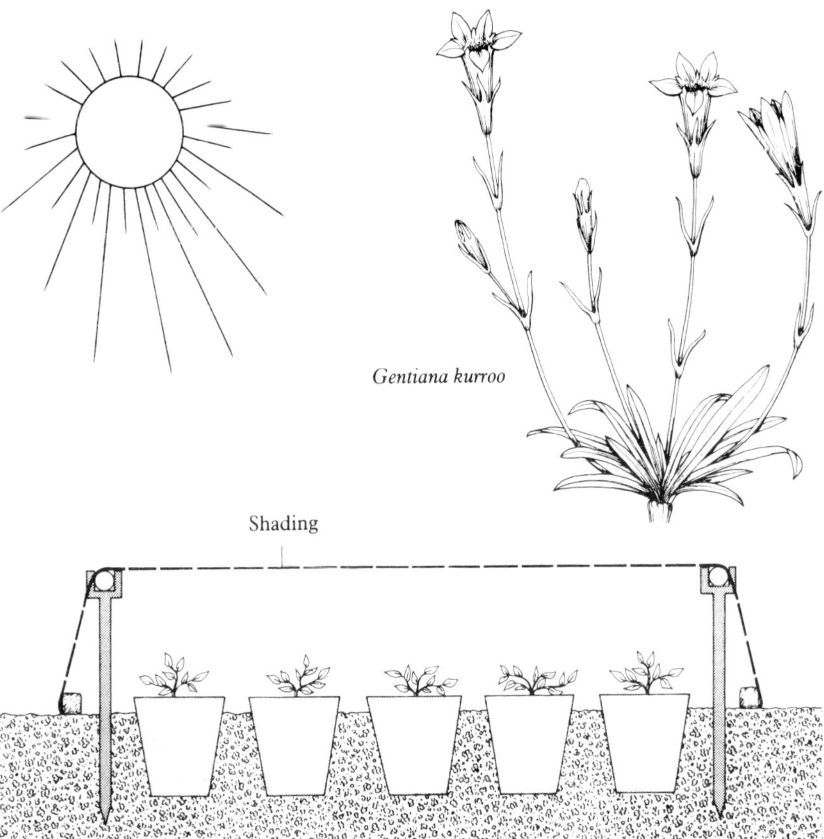

Young gentian plants must be protected from strong sunlight

Figure 8 Shading young gentian plants

G. *sceptrum* Likes compost rich in humus, but is lime loving.

G. *septemfida* Best results from sowing in August–September.

G. *septemfida* var. *lagodechiana* Prefers soil rich in humus, but is not a lime hater. Seedlings vary markedly.

G. *setigera* Normal compost, keep moist; tolerates lime.

G. *stragulata* Very seldom sets seed.

G. *trichotoma* Sow in peaty compost in January–February. Lime free.

G. *waltonii* Presents no difficulties. Sow in winter in ordinary compost.

After germination, further development is very slow. Depending on the species, two to seven years may be needed before the plants are ready to flower. The compost in the pots used for pricking out must be much more carefully adjusted to meet the later requirements of the plant.

Gentian seeds are not always easy to procure. Because of the opportunities for early sowing, seed harvested by the gardener himself is particularly valuable. The seed heads should be harvested just before they are ripe and kept in a dry place inside the house so that the seeds can fall out on to a sheet of paper. Orders should be sent to seed suppliers as early as possible.

Propagation by division

As compared with other genera of garden perennials, there are relatively few gentians which can be propagated by division. Many of them have only a single tap root or a compact root system united in a single root head.

Nevertheless, the various species of spring-flowering trumpet gentian are suitable for division. A large, well-established mat should be chosen for the purpose. The plant should be carefully dug up with a fork and cut with a spade or knife into two or three fair-sized pieces. Alternatively, the gardener can take a few individual rosettes, each with a piece of root, and plant them in the place where they are intended to remain, though it is often better, especially in light soils, to grow on these little plants in pots for a time. Once they have made good root growth they can be planted out. The best time for division is June, whether the species is *G. acaulis*, *G. alpina*, *G. clusii*, *G. angustifolia* or *G. dinarica*.

Only in the rarest instances do *G. verna* and its relatives *G. verna* var. *angulosa* and *G. verna* var. *oschtenica* form mats large enough to be divided without fear of loss. The time for division is the same as for the *acaulis* group.

Most of the autumn-flowering Asiatic gentians can also be divided. As flowering comes to an end, young shoots will appear at the base of the plant. Cut away the old shoots which have finished flowering, dig up the plant and divide the clump of young shoots. If it is to be replanted immediately, divide it into only two or three parts, but if pot propagation is feasible single shoots can be planted. When dealing with very late-flowering species and varieties or in districts subject to early frosts, it may be better to carry out division in the spring. Specialists recommend February–March for *G. farreri* and April for *G. hexaphylla*.

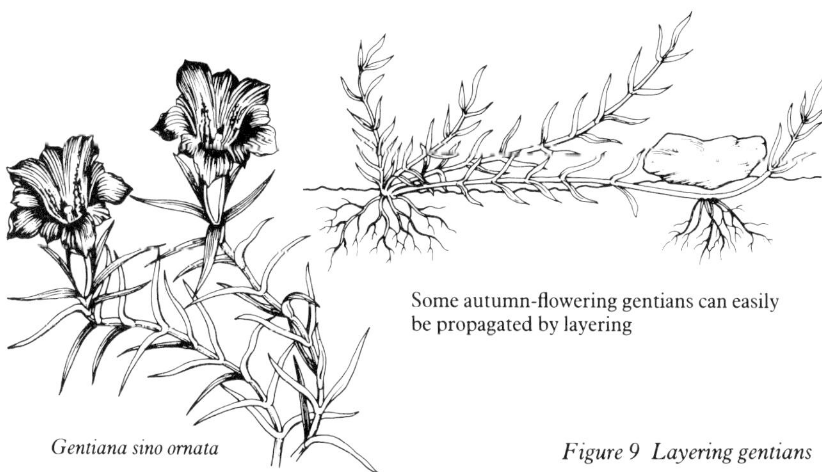
Gentiana sino ornata

Some autumn-flowering gentians can easily be propagated by layering

Figure 9 Layering gentians

Old plants of the willow gentian, *G. asclepiadea*, can often be successfully divided. It is important to make sure that each piece has an adequate amount of root and several growth buds. The plant should be divided in spring before the commencement of growth.

From time to time it may be possible to divide old plants of other species, though generally other modes of propagation are preferable. For example, when dealing with the summer-flowering species, old plants can be dug up with a fork in spring. Individual roots can be torn off from above in such a way that part of the head is taken with each. These pieces are then planted in deep pots and grown on.

Propagation by cuttings

Here one has to draw a line between what is feasible and what is worthwhile. The species and varieties of Chinese autumn-flowering gentians are customarily propagated by cuttings. Cuttings taken before flowering and put out in a moist compost of peat, leaf mould and sand, in half shade in a humid atmosphere will root swiftly. Rooting hormone is often quite unnecessary. Cuttings can be taken from *G. farreri*, the most lime-tolerant species of this group, from June to August. Good results are given by cuttings 5 to 6cm (just over 2 in) in length. Cuttings from *G. sino ornata* and *G. veitchiorum* should be taken by September. Cuttings from *G. hexaphylla* and *G. lawrencei* should be taken somewhat earlier, from June to August, though the latter species needs longer for rooting.

As regards the newer hybrids, the later their flowering time, the longer the period during which cuttings can be taken. Shoots with fully developed buds should never be used as cuttings.

Another mode of propagation for this group is layering. When the shoots are long enough, a small amount of humus-rich soil is piled over the middle of each shoot and topped with a small stone. The plant and its surroundings must not be allowed to get too dry. By autumn roots will have formed at the point where the shoot is in contact with the soil. The shoot is then cut off close to the roots and potted up. This method of propagation is particularly useful for the amateur.

Cuttings can also be taken from the spring gentians, both those of the *acaulis* group and *G. verna* and its relations. In these cases the cutting often has a few roots at the outset. June is the best time. Basal cuttings from *G. septemfida* and *G. septemfida* var. *lagodechiana* also root well.

There are of course many other species from which cuttings can be taken, but the yield is not high and the method is worthwhile only for

Plate 3

These colour photographs depict the wide range of plants available in the *acaulis* group.

Above: In the author's garden 'Angustifolia hybrid Frei' is the best cultivar of this group. It combines all their good qualities: it grows vigorously, flowers reliably and profusely, and carries large, brilliant-blue flowers on long stalks, long enough to serve as cut flowers for small bouquets.

Middle left: All albino forms are uncommon and much sought after by enthusiasts. *Gentiana alpina* 'Alba' is a true rarity.

Middle right: *G. acaulis* 'Alba' (syn. *G. kochiana* 'Alba') is somewhat more widely distributed. As it is a lime-hater, some thought must be given to the compost.

Below left: *G. alpina*, the gentian of the southern Alps, is distributed over a wide area but is nowhere very common. It is found chiefly in thin alpine turf on igneous rocks. In the garden, even when its soil requirements are carefully provided, it is far from easy to cultivate. Its flowers are prone to fungal rot.

Below right: the variety 'Coelestina' has large flowers of a blue from which any red tinge has been almost entirely eliminated.

enthusiasts. Early summer is the best time, and rooting hormones are useful. The part of the cutting buried in the compost (peat and sand) should always be carefully freed of leaves. Maintenance of adequate humidity is of course essential (cover with glass or transparent film). The temperature for rooting should not be too high: 15°C (60°F) is usually sufficient. The sand used in the compost is of great importance. It should be as sharp and crystalline as possible. 'Soft' sand with rounded granules or containing loam or clay is quite unsuitable.

Cultivation

As already noted, the members of this large genus have very different requirements as regards soil, soil reaction, position in the garden and other factors. However, there are some species which make no special demands, will grow in any kind of soil and flourish in most gardens, while others can be difficult to grow.

There are certain parts of the world where the climate, though unfavourable for many other garden plants, is peculiarly suitable for growing gentians. These areas are mainly alpine and alpine foot hills

Plate 4

Gentiana verna, the spring gentian, delights everyone who sees its large floral carpets in the wild. In the Alps and other European mountains this species often appears in large numbers soon after the snow thaw. Because of its wide distribution it has adapted to show some notable variation. Unfortunately, *G. verna* is difficult in the garden, never truly at home in cultivation and not very often seen.

Above left: A somewhat better garden plant is its variety from the Caucasus, *G. verna* var. *angulosa*.

Above right: *G. verna* var. *angulosa* (syn. *G. angulosa*) photographed in the wild in the Caucasus. The plants were growing in lava rubble with relatively little humus. (Mount Elbrus, mid-June, altitude approximately 2,800m (9,200 ft)).

Below: The spring gentian growing wild in the Alps. Where it grows the soil is usually rich in humus and saturated with water at flowering time. Deliberate selection might result in the emergence of forms better adapted to garden life.

(pre-Alpine region), central uplands and coastal districts. In Germany, the eastern part of upper Franconia is a good example. Nowhere can one see more luxuriant carpets of Asiatic autumn-flowering gentians than in Hof and Weiden, the coldest district of Germany, though the lime-free soil certainly makes a major contribution.

The essentials can be briefly summed up. Gentians need soil which is moist but not wet, good drainage, a certain minimum of atmospheric humidity, high light intensity and a place where the temperature is never unduly high. From this it will be obvious that any attempt to grow the more tricky species in districts with hot summers will run into difficulties. The warmer the climate, the greater the need for protection from sunlight, though the chosen place must not be dark. It may be a problem to combine high light intensity with a cool spot. The solution may be to choose a place in a small depression, in an open site, shaded from the hottest midday sun by conifers or dwarf deciduous shrubs. A garden layout with abundant relief offers more places for difficult gentian species than a completely flat piece of ground.

The composition of the soil requires more attention than is necessary for most small perennials. Even within the groups there are differences. For example, certain species of the *acaulis* group require an acid soil and others demand lime, while their hybrids will tolerate a wider pH range. Soil structure is also of some importance. The *acaulis* group prefer light loamy soils, while the North American species favour peaty soils. A mixture of fine peat, leaf mould and loamy sand is best for the North American species. Planted in full sun and provided with adequate soil moisture (but never stagnant wetness) they will flourish extremely well (*G. andrewsii*, *G. bracteosa*, *G. calycosa*, *G. parryi*, *G. sceptrum*). It should be mentioned that *G. andrewsii* prefers somewhat more shade (but not full shade).

The autumn-flowering Asiatic gentians also like a peaty soil, but it should contain a larger supply of minerals (a mixture of peat, leaf mould and acid loamy gravelly soil). They also need an open sunny position and a certain minimum of soil moisture. The pH should be on the acid side of neutral, but the species differ in their requirements. *G. sino ornata* is a rabid lime hater; *G. farreri* will tolerate some lime, and the others lie between these two extremes (*G. hexaphylla*, *G. ornata*, *G. prolata*, etc.).

There are some summer-flowering Asiatic gentians which like lime, but can flourish without it provided the soil is not too acid (*G. decumbens*, *G. dahurica*, *G. tianshanica*). The tall European species such as *G. lutea*, *G. punctata*, *G. purpurea* and their hybrids are not particular about the soil, provided it is deep enough to accommodate their long roots. It need not be cultivated topsoil for the entire depth, but there

In limestone districts, certain additives can be incorporated in the compost and the water used for irrigation to maintain an acid soil reaction:

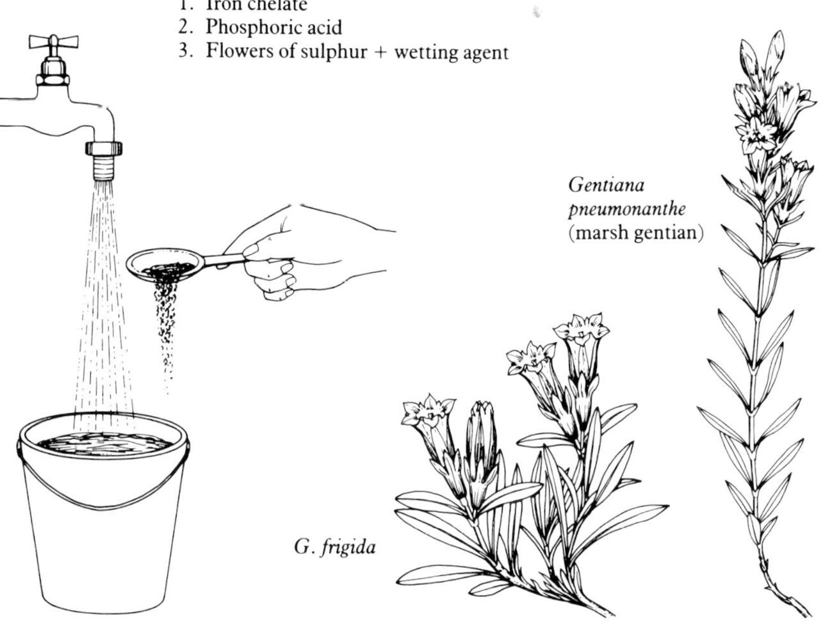

Figure 10 Maintaining acid soil reaction

must not be a layer of stone or solid clay to block the downward growth of the roots. In very warm situations partial shade may be beneficial. Other species which are happy in any reasonable soil, provided it is retentive of moisture yet well drained, include *G. cephalantha*, *G. freyniana*, *G. scabra*, *G. septemfida*, *G. septemfida* var. *lagodechiana* and their forms and hybrids.

These brief hints are as much as can be given here. Further details will be found under the descriptions of the species. For example, the grower can be guided by the fact that *G. sino ornata* grows in China on peaty, acid soil, *G. verna* in Europe on limestone subsoil, *G. glauca* in Japan on volcanic ash, and *G. saxosa* on sandhills on the coast of New Zealand.

Manuring plays a smaller part than with certain other genera. Care must always be taken to avoid over-manuring, although some of the less fastidious species will tolerate substantial doses of fertiliser, either mineral or organic. Normally it is enough to give a light top-dressing once a year, consisting of peat and sand in equal parts mixed with a small proportion of fine horn chips. For species which do not require a highly acid soil the horn chips can be replaced by Peru guano. However, it must be remembered that horn chips provide a gentle, long-lasting fertiliser action, while Peru guano has potent but short-lasting effects; this must be remembered when selecting the dose. On acid soils a peat-based rhododendron fertiliser mixed with sand may be used. In limestone districts, if signs of chlorosis appear despite the application of peat in the annual top dressing, organic iron-chelate preparations (Sequestrene) will be helpful. These supplements are most effective if applied in February or March during wet weather. In dry weather they must be washed in by adequate watering. These products are in part taken up directly through the leaves, but if used for this purpose they must not be too concentrated.

Careful attention must be given to the water used for watering or irrigation. Water companies will generally let you know the degree of hardness of their mains water. Hard water is unsuitable for exacting species which demand an acid soil. The usual remedy is to collect rain water. In industrial areas this is not without problems of its own. If mains water has to be used, chelated iron should be added. It may be helpful to add a little phosphoric acid to the water, or to put the water in a barrel or some other container and immerse in it a small sack filled with peat. All these measures are intended to ensure that the plant receives its vital supplies of iron, the place of which would otherwise be occupied by calcium.

The techniques for planting gentians are much the same as for other small perennials. In most cases the gardener will be dealing with plants with root-balls (container-grown plants). Even those plants which have been raised at home from seed or cuttings will usually have been grown on for a time in pots. This means that plants can be put out in the garden at practically any time of year, though in general spring or autumn planting is preferable. All other things being equal, spring planting is better. Autumn planting involves some danger that the root-balls may be dislodged by frost unless they are firmly anchored in the surrounding earth. The root-balls of pot-grown gentians do not have as many fibrous roots as those of other genera, and therefore break up more readily when removed from their pots. The gardener must therefore take extra care, and must see that the root-balls are thoroughly moistened beforehand. Loose planting must be avoided, in other words the root-balls must be firmly pressed down and the surrounding soil must be firmly packed round them. After planting out the young plants should be thoroughly watered, and if sunny weather follows this watering must be repeated.

The care of gentians outside their flowering season presents no special difficulties. They need watering during prolonged dry spells. Dead flowers may be removed, but this is not essential. Tidying up and the removal of dead growth should be left till the spring, and should not be done until new basal shoots are clearly visible. It goes without saying that the plantings must be kept weed free. It is a good idea to keep a few home-propagated gentians in small pots as a reserve, not only to make good any losses but also to provide gifts for other gentian enthusiasts.

Pests and diseases

In contrast to certain other plants, gentians are relatively seldom affected by pests or diseases. From time to time, however, cuttings or even seedlings may be destroyed by fungus diseases, leaves become discoloured and spotted, and buds are attacked by insects or moulds. It is a well-known fact that healthy vigorous plants which have been well cultivated are less prone to attack by pests and diseases than those which struggle to survive in unsuitable positions.

Slugs and snails In the writer's garden it is always slugs and snails which cause the most damage. When they become too numerous counter measures must be taken. Nibbled leaves and buds are signs of their presence, as are the well-known slime trails. Under ideal conditions they would be eaten by other residents of the garden—hedgehogs and toads. In the absence of such allies we are driven back on the conventional remedies: slug pellets, slug traps baited with beer, potatoes cut in half and laid on the ground to be collected every morning, and other methods of varying effectiveness.

Ants These are troublesome rather than harmful. The old household remedy of pouring boiling water into their nests is impracticable because it would destroy the gentians as well as the ants. If they are extremely troublesome one of the commercial ant killers may be tried.

Thrips Plants are occasionally infested by thrips, tiny insects which sometimes appear in large numbers in warm weather. Thrips suck juice from leaves and flowers, producing characteristic mottling and discoloration. Repeated spraying with a suitable insecticide may be of some help.

Caterpillars Certain caterpillars (larvae of butterflies and beetles) are sometimes a hazard to germinating seed and young plants. The remedy is to spray with one of the approved insecticides at 10-day intervals.

Eelworm Can be recognised from the slight distortion of the upper leaves (similar to that seen in summer-flowering phlox) and the arrested (deformed) growth of the plants. The only remedy is to spray three times at ten-day intervals with E 605, Perfekthion, Nemafos or Metasystox.

Grey mould (*Botrytis cinerea*) Of all the fungal diseases which attack gentians this is one of the most difficult to control. The signs of infection are most easily recognised in the flowers. Greyish-brown spots appear on them, and during persistently wet weather the condition worsens. A layer of grey mildew often becomes visible at spots where the fungus has been established for some time. The trouble is most likely to arise in poorly ventilated cold frames and alpine houses. Remove affected shoots immediately. The trouble can be prevented by spraying or dusting with a fungicide. A buoyant atmosphere, without stuffiness, is still the best protection.

Leafspot (*Septoria*) Small yellowish brown spots with violet edges appear on the leaves, chiefly towards their tips. The best remedy is a copper preparation such as Bordeaux mixture.

Gentian rust (*Puccinia gentianae*) This rust fungus, specific to gentians, is highly resistant to chemical fungicides. Dark brown pustules appear on the leaves; severe infection can even prove fatal to the plant. The affected parts of the plant should be cut off and burnt; on no account throw them on the compost heap. After dealing with an outbreak take care not to plant gentians in the same spot for several years.

Basal rot Especially during warm moist weather, the stems may rot off at the base, particularly in autumn-flowering Asiatic species and varieties. The best preventive measure is to dust the base of the plant with a Zineb preparation. Under conditions of warmth and moisture this fungus can cause great destruction among seedlings; the only remedy is to use sterilised seed compost and carefully cleaned seed pans. Though high humidity is necessary for seedlings, it is essential to prevent water dripping on to them from the glass or film used to cover the seed boxes. This can best be avoided by setting the covering material at a slight angle.

Viruses A few instances of virus infection have been noted. It is uncertain whether the virus is specific to gentians or whether it is one which also affects other genera. Propagation by seed reduces the risk of virus infection but does not entirely exclude it. Spots and other areas of discoloration on the leaves or other parts of the plant may be due to viruses, but may also be caused by other micro-organisms and plant diseases or even by unsatisfactory cultivation.

The Classification of Gentians

Taxonomy and classification

The classification of the genus *Gentiana* began relatively early and goes back to the first names in Reneaulme's *Specimen historiae plantarum* (1611). Further attempts appeared in Linnaeus' *Species plantarum* (1753), Necker's *Elementa botanica* (1790) and Froelich's *De Gentiana libellus sistens* (1796). Froelich's classification was accepted, with minor modifications, by Lamarck and de Candolle in 1805 and used in the *Flora Française*. This was the first work in which the genus was subdivided into sections in the present sense of the word. Another writer who studied the question was Link (*Enumeratio* 1821–2 and *Hortus Regius* 1829–33). Dumortier divided the genus into five sections in his *Florula Belgica* (1827). Further breakdown into ten subdivisions followed in Gaudin's *Flora Helvetica* (1828–1833).

Bunge's monograph on the gentian (1829), Grisebach's review of Gentianaceae in Hooker's *Flora Boreali-Americanae* and Grisebach's two major treatises on Gentianaceae (1838 and 1845) resulted in an overall classification which approached more closely to modern ideas. The most up-to-date classification of the entire genus is the one undertaken by Kusnezow. His monograph entitled *Subgenus Eugentiana* (1894) and his chapter on gentians in 'Die natürliche Pflanzenfamilien' (1895) are today still the basis of the taxonomy and classification of the genus.

Although Kusnezow's classification has many shortcomings, with the exception of C. V. B. Marquand's work, there is unfortunately little in the way of an up-to-date work which includes the numerous new species discovered since Kusnezow's time. The following review of the genus is based on the classification by Kusnezow; the species which he listed are printed in bold type and those added later in italics.

Section I — Coelanthe (Gentiana): **G. lutea**, **G. purpurea**, *G. punctata*, *G. pannonica*, *G. burseri*

Section II — Pneumonanthe: **G. andrewsii**, **G. makinoi**, **G. pneumonanthe**, **G. asclepiadea**, *G. scabra*, *G. gelida*, *G. jesoana*, *G. calycosa*, *G. newberryi*, *G. septemfida*, *G. bisetaea*, *G. freyniana*, *G. parryi*, *G. autumnalis*, *G. sceptrum*, *G. triflora*, *G. puberulenta*,

	G. catesbaei, *G. saponaria*, *G. decora*, *G. austromontana*, *G. clausa*, *G. linearis*, *G. rubicaulis*, *G. alba*, *G. villosa*
Section III	Otophora: **G. otophora**, *G. damionensis*
Section IV	Stenogyne: **G. rhodanta**, **G. stricta**, *G. pterocalyx* (annual)
Section V	Frigida: **G. chinensis**, **G. frigida**, *G. hexaphylla*, *G. veitchiorum*, *G. prolata*, *G. ornata*, *G. sino ornata*, *G. lawrencei*, *G. farreri*, *G. georgei*, *G. przewalskii*, *G. froelichii*, *G. glauca*, *G. stragulata*, *G. tubiflora*
Section VI	Aperta (Cruciata): **G. cruciata**, **G. decumbens**, *G. waltonii*, *G. gracilipes*, *G. tibetica*, *G. kurroo*, *G. crassicaulis*, *G. straminea*, *G. bigelovi*, *G. dendrologii*, *G. dahurica*, *G. grombczewskii*, *G. macrophylla*, *G. wutaiensis*, *G. fetisowii*, *G. walujewii* var. *kesselringii*
Section VII	Isomeria: **G. loderi**, *G. cachemirica*, *G. depressa*
Section VIII	Chondrophylla: **G. altaica**, **G. squarrosa**, *G. prostrata*, *G. pyrenaica*, *G. nipponica*, *G. boryi*
Section IX	Thylacites (Megalanthe): **G. acaulis**, *G. alpina*, *G. angustifolia*, *G. clusii*, *G. dinarica*, *G. ligustica*, *G. occidentalis*
Section X	Cyclostigma (Calathianae): **G. nivalis**, **G. verna**, *G. bavarica*, *G. brachyphylla*, *G. pumila*, *G. rostanii*, *G. terglouensis*, *G. utriculosa*, *G. orbicularis*

Kusnezow divided the genus *Gentiana* into two subgenera, *Eugentiana* and *Gentianella*, and subdivided these subgenera into 19 sections. The splitting off of *Gentianella* and *Gentianopsis* into two independent genera left only the ten sections listed above, but the classification is still of value even today as a guide to natural affinities. The New Zealand species are classified in Subgenus 2. *Gentianella*. Section 12: Andicola.

In volume 3 of *Flora Europaea* the European species of gentian are listed as follows:

Section I	Gentiana: *G. lutea*, *G. punctata*, *G. pannonica*, *G. purpurea*, *G. burseri*
Section II	Pneumonanthe: *G. asclepiadea*, *G. pneumonanthe*
Section III	Frigida: *G. frigida*, *G. froelichii*

Section IV Cruciata: *G. cruciata*, *G. decumbens*

Section V Chondrophyllae: *G. prostrata*, *G. pyrenaica*, *G. boryi*, *G. septemfida*

Section VI Megalanthae (Thylacites): *G. acaulis*, *G. clusii*, *G. occidentalis*, *G. ligustica*, *G. alpina*, *G. dinarica*, *G. angustifolia*

Section VII Calathianae: *G. verna*, *G. brachyphylla*, *G. pumila*, *G. bavaria*, *G. rostanii*, *G. terglouensis*, *G. nivalis*, *G. utriculosa*

Various older classifications are still to be found. For example, in the article entitled 'Species of Gentian from China and the Himalayas' by C. V. B. Marquand in the *Journal of the Royal Horticultural Society* (vol. 57, September 1932) the species are divided as follows:

Section I Otophora: *G. damyonensis*

Section II Stenogyne: *G. pterocalyx* (annual)

Section III Dipterospermum: *G. helenii*

Section IV Tripterospermum: *G. golowninia*

Section V Frigida: *G. hexaphylla*, *G. setulifolia*, *G. veitchiorum*, *G. prolata*, *G. ornata*, *G. sino ornata*, *G. lawrencei*, *G. namlaensis*, *G. farreri*, *G. georgei*, *G. stragulata*, *G. sikkimensis*, *G. rigescens*, *G. trichotoma*, *G. przewalskii*, *G. praeclara* (annual), *G. picta* (annual)

Section VI Aperta: *G. waltonii*, *G. gracilipes*, *G. tibetica*, *G. robusta*, *G. kurroo*, *G. crassicaulis*, *G. straminea*

Section VII Pneumonanthe: *G. scabra*

Section VIII Isomeria: *G. delavayi* (annual), *G. cachemirica*, *G. loderi*, *G. chondrophylla*

Section IX No designation given: *G. moniliformis*, *G. crassuloides*, *G. pentastica* (all annual)

The gentians of Japan have been reviewed by Dr Toyokumi in his monograph.

In this short account it is impossible to go into the reasons for the repeated subdivisions into separate groups or sections, their promotion to independent genera and, in some instances, their subsequent re-incorporation. (*Crawfurdia* Wall., *Gentianella* Moench, *Megacodon* (Hemsl.) H. Sm., *Tripterospermum* Blune, *Comastoma* (Wettst.) Toyokumi, *Gentianopsis* Ma and *Pterygocalyx* Maxim.). Taxonomic work of this kind will certainly continue, and although it may be of scientific value it tends to be irritating and troublesome to those who are interested in gentians purely as garden plants. The genera with which we are concerned in this book are

Gentiana L.
Gentianella Moench
Gentianopsis Ma

The best-known and important species of gentian

Gentiana acaulis L. (trumpet gentian)

SYNONYMS: *G. excisa* W. D. J. Koch non K. B. Presl., *G. kochiana* Perr. et Song., *Ericoila kochiana* (Perr. et Song.) A. et D. Löve

To avoid confusion it should be said that the gentian described here is the species long known as *G. kochiana*. The name *G. acaulis* was widely used as a collective designation, as was the German name 'Stengeloser Enzian' (stemless gentian).

There are clear morphological distinctions between these three and they are likely to maintain their status in time to come. However, there are certain authors who propose to merge the genus *Gentianopsis* in *Gentianella*. The writer does not adopt this view.

Much work has recently been carried out in Canada by Dr James S. Pringle of the Royal Botanical Garden, Hamilton, Ontario. He has not proposed a new overall classification, but in his privately printed study *Sectional and Subgeneric names in Gentiana (Gentianaceae)* all previously recognised sections—valid or invalid—are treated in detail, though without any definitive appraisal.

However, Dr Pringle has published revised classifications of the species of Section Pneumonanthe found in north-eastern North America, Mexico and Central America. A monograph on the gentians (*Gentianella* ssp.) of Equador has appeared and further monographs on the gentians of Peru and Western America are planned.

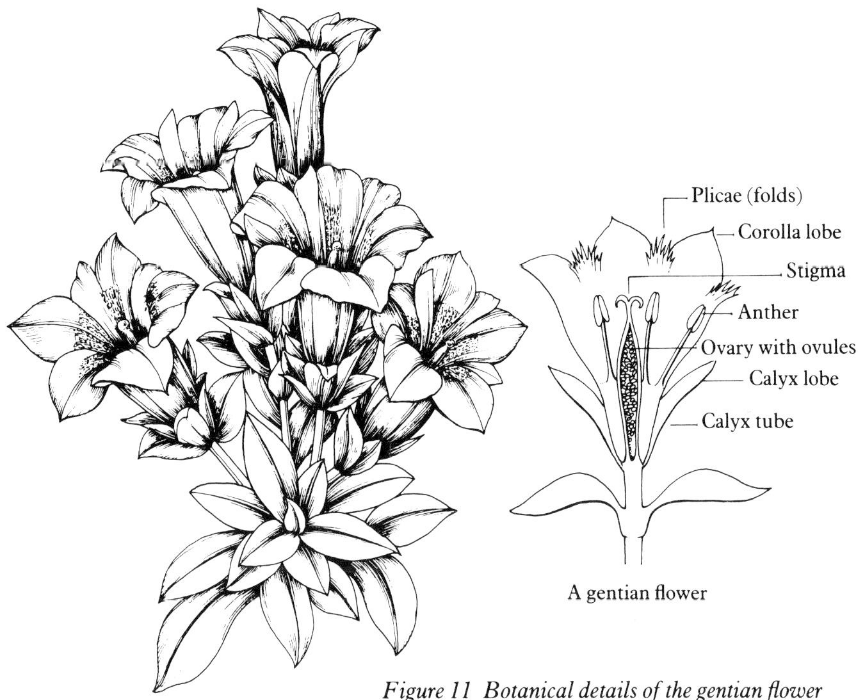

Figure 11 Botanical details of the gentian flower

Gentiana acaulis

Nowadays it is permissible to use the term '*acaulis* group', which comprises the following species:

G. acaulis L.
G. alpina Vill.
G. angustifolia Vill.
G. clusii Perr. et Song.
G. dinarica Beck
G. ligustica R. de Vilmorin et Chopinet
G. occidentalis Jakowatz.

Flora Europaea gives the following key:

1 Mature rosette-leaves scarcely longer than wide *G. alpina*
1 Mature rosette-leaves at least 1½ times as long as wide
2 Mature rosette-leaves linear-oblanceolate to oblanceolate *G. angustifolia*

2 Mature rosette-leaves lanceolate, elliptical or obovate
3 Calyx-teeth triangular, widest at base, usually more than ½ as long as the tube *G. clusii*
3 Calyx-teeth lanceolate to ovate, narrowed at base
4 Corolla with green spots in the throat; calyx-teeth usually less than ½ as long as the tube
5 Calyx-teeth about 1½ times as long as wide; corolla-lobes acute or cuspidate *G. acaulis*
5 Calyx-teeth little longer than wide; corolla-lobes acuminate *G. ligustica*
4 Corolla nearly or quite without green spots in the throat; calyx-teeth usually at least ½ as long as the tube
6 Calyx-teeth usually more than ½ as long as the tube; corolla-lobes acute *G. occidentalis*
6 Calyx-teeth about ½ as long as the tube; corolla-lobes acuminate *G. dinarica*

Now to *G. acaulis* itself. It has a wide distribution over the mountains of Southern Europe including the Alps (from the Dauphiné to Carinthia), Pyrenees, Jura, Carpathians, and Balkans (Yugoslavia and Bulgaria). In Germany it is found in the Bavarian Alps and the Allgäu but not in the Berchtesgaden Alps. Although generally preferring igneous or acid rocks, it is not as fastidious as some of its close relatives and is also to be found on chalky limestone, marl, slate, conglomerate and sandstone. It grows mainly on dry turf and pastures, rubble and scree slopes and even in alpine and subalpine coniferous woods at altitudes of 1,700 to 3,000m (5,500 to 9,800 ft). It must have a certain minimum of fine loamy or peaty soil. In nature its associates include *Rhododendron ferrugineum*, *Geum montanum*, *Campanula barbata* and *Chrysanthemum alpinum*, and these go well with it in the garden.

This perennial gentian forms a rosette of smooth, hairless matt-green leaves, above which are one or two pairs of stem leaves arising from a very short scape. The basal leaves are elliptic-oval, ovate or more rarely obovate, 4 to 15cm (1⅝ to 6 in) long and two to three times longer than broad. The bell-shaped flower is comparatively large, measuring up to 6cm (2⅜ in). The calyx is bell shaped, five toothed, the rounded calyx teeth being less than half as long as the calyx tube; they diverge outwards from the corolla and the broad spaces between the calyx lobes are filled by white, connecting membranes. The funnel-shaped to bell-shaped corolla is normally a deep sky-blue, though violet, reddish-violet, greenish-white and white forms can be found here and there. There are olive-green spots in the throat. The golden-yellow anthers are a striking feature, as is the style with its fringed stigmata. In nature the flowering season extends from June to August. Renewed flowering in autumn is unusual.

The true botanical species are of little value to the ordinary gardener, as they often fail to grow or flower well in lowland gardens. However, certain splendid strains of trumpet gentian have long been cultivated —in Europe, certainly since the time of Louis XIV (1638–1714). The result has been an aggregate involving various species and varieties of the *acaulis* group. Gardeners have selected the most vigorous and floriferous seedlings, and have propagated them vegetatively. Today there are still various strains, and as their origins are uncertain they are discussed under the heading 'Hybrids'.

Specialists will of course wish to cultivate the true species as well, one of the most sought after being the albino form (*G. acaulis* 'Alba').

In the garden it should be given a loamy soil with plenty of humus and a slightly acid reaction; some non-calcareous grit can be added. The site should be sunny or half shaded and a reasonable degree of moisture should be ensured. In the garden it needs moister soil than in nature so as to compensate for the lower humidity. Though coming chiefly from the Central Alps the species is reasonably lime tolerant; it is not such a confirmed lime hater as *G. sino ornata*. Even in favourable sites it does not flower profusely; if it ceases to flower altogether it should be divided and the pieces replanted elsewhere. Feeding should be extremely cautious: as little as 0.25g of artificial fertiliser in 1 litre (1⁄10 oz in 1 pt) of water can be harmful.

Among suitable associates are *Primula auricula*, *Alchemilla hoppeana*, *Leontopodium* species and varieties, and *Arnebia pulchra* (*A. echioides*). In the garden-plant trials this species has been assigned to the category of plants for the enthusiast.

Gentiana affinis Griseb.

In publications from the USA this is often listed as *Pneumonanthe affinis* (Griseb.) Green.

It has a wide distribution in North America, ranging from Saskatchewan, Manitoba and North Dakota as far as British Columbia and southwards to Nevada, Arizona and the rocky hills of New Mexico. It grows mainly in the lower foothills of the main ranges, on moist, mildly acid soil.

It is an erect plant about 30cm (12 in) tall with leafy stems, the upper stem leaves, obovate to oblong, being narrower and more sharply pointed than the lower. Each flower scape carries two or three flowers (sometimes more) in the upper leaf axils. The uppermost or terminal flower is sessile, while those arising from the leaf axils are usually stalked. The flowering season extends from July to August or from August to September depending on location. The calyx lobes vary in size, often being up to 6cm (2⅜ in) long.

The narrow, funnel-shaped flowers are 2.5cm (1 in) in length or a little more, and are blue in colour though their hue may vary. The corolla lobes are ovate, divergent and considerably longer than the plicae, which are usually split into two or three segments.

There is some disagreement regarding its value as a garden plant, probably because various different forms have been distributed. Nevertheless, it deserves a place in the garden, even though it is not among the finest of American plants and will never attract swarms of admirers. It

Plate 5

The *Verna* group comprises some delightful wild flowers, but none of them are easy garden plants; at best, they are the carefully guarded treasures of the specialist alpine gardener.

Above left: Among the most sought after rarities is *Gentiana verna* var. *oschtenica* (syn. *G. oschtenica*), a yellow-flowered form of the spring gentian from the Caucasus. In cultivation it is even more difficult than the blue-flowered forms.

Above right: The Triglav gentian, *G. terglouensis*, grows mainly on limestone soils. Though seldom offered it is one of the species of this group which is comparatively easy in cultivation, given appropriate care.

Middle left: The snow gentian, *G. nivalis*, is hardly ever encountered in cultivation, even under alpine-house conditions. This miniature species grows in many mountain ranges, usually at moderate altitudes, and is also found in Greenland.

Middle right: *G. utriculosa* is another plant to be enjoyed when found in the wild; attempts at cultivation are unlikely to be successful.

Below left: *G. bavarica*, the Bavarian gentian, differs from the spring gentian mainly in the shape of its leaves.

Below right: *G. pumila*, the dwarf gentian. By giving special attention to its requirements, some specialists have been able to grow this species satisfactorily.

needs a place in full sun, with reasonably damp soil yet without stagnant moisture. In nature it grows in association with *Potentilla fruticosa*, a partnership equally appropriate in the garden. It also consorts well with hardy fuchsias (*Fuchsia magellanica*). *G. affinis* is closely related to *G. forwoodii*, *G. interrupta*, *G. bigelovii* and certain others, though it is uncertain whether all these deserve the status of separate species. It is propagated by seed.

Gentiana alba Mühlenb

SYNONYM: *G. flavida* A. Gray

A North American species found in the central states of the USA and in Canada, chiefly in southern Michigan, in central Minnesota extending southwards to Kentucky, in north-west Arkansas, in eastern Kansas and in scattered localities as far as southern Virginia and western North

Plate 6

These photographs show that the genus *Gentian* is not restricted to low-growing species and that it has flowers of other colours than blue. These tall gentians are suitable for the large rock garden and for the wild garden, though patience is necessary, as young plants require several years before reaching flowering size.

Above left and above right: *Gentiana lutea*, the yellow gentian, has been used for medicinal purposes since antiquity; the thick roots are also the raw material for the well-known gentian schnaps. In suitable spots in the garden this tall, long-lived perennial is highly decorative.

Centre right: *G. pannonica*, the Hungarian gentian, is not restricted to Hungary, but widely distributed in the mountains of Central Europe. Though not of outstanding garden merit, it is not without a certain charm.

Below left: *G. purpurea*, the purple gentian, is more attractive than *G. pannonica* and welcome in the garden; however, it requires lime-free soil. As it does not exceed 45cm (18 in) in height it is suitable for the smaller rock garden.

Below right: *G.* × *kummeriana* is a rare hybrid between *G. lutea* × *G. pannonica*, the colour of its flowers betraying its ancestry.

Carolina. It grows in the prairies, in places that are not too dry, and in meadowland in low-hill country.

A robust, erect, unbranched plant some 60 to 80cm (2 to 2½ ft) tall. Leaves ovate to lanceolate, arranged in pairs on the stem, 7 to 12cm (2¾ to 4¾ in) long and roughly 2.5cm (1 in) broad. They are cordate at the base and drawn out to a point at the tip, with smooth margins. The flowers are held in a large, terminal cluster, and are sessile or very short stalked. The individual blooms are whitish, marked with greenish or yellowish veins, tubular and 3 to 5cm (1³⁄₁₆ to 2 in) long. They have some resemblance to those of *G. saponaria* (*G. puberula*) but are more open and bell shaped. The corolla lobes are oblong-ovate and more than twice as long as the irregular and toothed plicae. It flowers in August to September.

This gentian is hardly a match for others of its genus. Though a vigorous grower, its attractiveness is limited, and it is of interest only to the collector or the botanist. Unfortunately, all kinds of other species masquerade under the name of *G. alba* in collected material and seed exchanges. It might be rewarding to make large sowings and select the most pleasing types.

In the garden this species requires lime-free soil, with a reasonable amount of moisture and an open site.

Gentiana algida Pallas.

SYNONYMS: *G. algida* var. *sibirica* Kusn., G. *nubigena* Edgew., *G. romanzovii* Ledeb. ex Bunge, *G. frigida* var. *algida* (Pall.) Froel.

A wide-ranging species, occurring in eastern Asia and in North America. It has been found in eastern Siberia, south-western China, Japan, Kashmir, Alaska, the western Yukon and in a few places in Montana, Wyoming and Colorado. Also known from the Aleutian Islands. Grows on hillsides in rather dry sites.

In consequence of its wide range the plant varies considerably. It is an attractive perennial, forming loose clumps 8 to 30cm (3³⁄₁₆ to 12 in) tall. The stems are angulated and greenish-yellow. The basal leaves are spatulate to linear, blunt, thick and fleshy, 2.5 to 5cm (1 to 2 in) long. The stem leaves are lanceolate and shorter (approx. 3.7cm) (1½ in). The rootstock is often covered with the remains of old basal leaves. The flowers are yellowish-white with blue spots and have blue ribs externally. They are borne in stalked clusters of one to three flowers, either in the leaf axils or terminally. They are tubular to bell shaped, the corolla being 3.5 to 4.5cm (1⅜ to 1¾ in) long. The corolla segments are erect, triangular and widely divergent. The calyx tube is 2cm (¾ in) long. Flowering time is August to September.

In cultivation it is often confused with the similar *G. frigida*, and some botanists regard *G. algida* as a variety of the latter. *G. algida* is a thoroughly attractive garden plant, though somewhat difficult. An artificial scree with highly efficient drainage is essential. A somewhat larger form with most attractive flowers up to 5cm (2 in) long, known as *G. igarashii* Miyabe et Kudo, comes from Central Honshu in Japan. Botanically, its correct name is *G. algida* var. *igarashii* Miyabe et Kudo. The Himalayan form is also known as *G. algida* var. *nubigena* (Edgew.) Kusn. It is easily raised from seed. The low-growing forms are suitable for troughs.

Gentiana alpina Vill., (southern alpine gentian)

SYNONYM: *G. acaulis* L. var *alpina* (Vill.) Griseb.

Widely distributed, though absent from Germany and Austria. Found in the Sierra Nevada, the Pyrenees, the Savoy Alps and the south-western Swiss Alps.

Not very common, it is confined mainly to sparse turf, on igneous rock. Most of its associates in nature are unsuitable for the garden, either because they are unattractive or because they are difficult plants such as *Eritrichium manum* or *Viola calcarata*.

It is a relatively compact representative of the *acaulis* group, growing to a height of 4 to 7cm (1⅝ to 2¾ in). The basal rosette is glabrous, the rootstock is short and the scape only 0.3 to 1cm (⅛ to ⅜ in) long or totally absent. The basal leaves are comparatively small and obtuse (a distinguishing feature from other species of the *acaulis* group), broad elliptic, leathery, matt green, 1.5 to 3cm (⅝ to 1 in) long (occasionally up to 4cm (1⅝ in)) and only slightly longer than broad. The stem leaves —not always present—are acutely elliptic to lanceolate and 0.9 to 1.4cm (⅜ to 9/16 in) long. The five-toothed calyx is bell shaped. The calyx lobes are roughly half the length of the calyx tube. The funnel-shaped to bell-shaped corolla is 3 to 4cm (1 3/16 to 1⅝ in) long, dark sky-blue with greenish spots, somewhat paler in the throat. Violet or white forms are occasionally found. The corolla lobes are slightly rounded. The flowering season in the wild is from June to August, in the garden usually June to July.

This species is more difficult in cultivation than *G. acaulis*. Given lime-free soil it will often grow well, but flowers sparsely or not at all. The soil should be kept slightly damp, yet good drainage is essential; stagnant moisture must be avoided. Nevertheless, it is an attractive plant, worthy of some trouble. Raising plants from seed calls for patience, as even fresh seed often fails to germinate until the second year after sowing.

Gentiana altaica Laxm.

Its home is Siberia, especially the Altai region, but it also occurs in the Baikal mountains and northern Mongolia. A tufted plant, it forms leafy shoots which resemble lax rosettes. In most instances each shoot bears only a single terminal flower, but occasionally there may be more. At the base of the flower the leaves—over 2.5cm (1 in) long—overlap closely; in shape they are linear to linear-lanceolate. The funnel-shaped, deep-blue flowers are more than 4cm (1½ in) long and almost 2cm (¾ in) broad when fully open. The corolla lobes are rounded to ovate and almost twice as long as the plicae. The latter are rounded and deeply notched. The corolla is paler in colour within. Flowering season May and June.

An excellent garden plant, though not widely grown. It requires rather stony soil and good drainage. During wet winter weather it is advisable to cover the plant with a sheet of glass or plastic. It needs a site in full sun. It is propagated by seed.

Gentiana amabilis Petrie

New Zealand (Central Otago 1,400m (4,500 ft)). Its specific status is perhaps unjustified, as it is probably a dwarf form of *G. bellidifolia*. The scapes, 4 to 5cm (1⅝ to 2 in) tall, bear a single, relatively large, terminal white flower. In the mountains of Central Otago it grows in association with *G. bellidifolia*, which normally prefers drier sites than the dwarf form distributed under the name of *G. amabilis*.

Gentiana amoena C. B. Clark

Sikkim Himalaya, at altitudes above 4500m (14,750 ft). A pretty, mat-forming species with closely overlapping leaves and long runners which carry bell-shaped terminal flowers of white or flesh-coloured tones, pencilled with longitudinal markings in dark blue. Unfortunately it is not in cultivation, though to judge from the illustration in David Wilkie's book *Gentians* (1936), it must be a desirable plant. It was introduced earlier in this century but lost during World War II. In the wild it flowers from August to October. It needs slightly moist soil of acid pH. Its re-introduction is to be desired.

Gentiana andrewsii Griseb. (closed gentian, blind gentian)

SYNONYMS: *Dasystephana andrewsii* (Griseb.) Small., *Pneumonanthe andrewsii* (Griseb.) W. A. Weber.

Its homeland is in the north-eastern states of the USA and the adjacent parts of Canada (Vermont and Quebec to Saskatchewan and southwards as far as Georgia, Arkansas and Colorado). It grows in moist woods and meadows. A central rootstock puts forth several leafy stems usually some 35cm (15 in) tall, but sometimes up to 80cm (2 ft 8 in). The stem leaves are paired, dark green, sometimes with a violet tinge, lanceolate to ovate, about 5cm (2 in) long and slightly more than half as wide, with three to seven veins. The flowers are terminal or may be situated in the upper leaf axils, where they form clusters. The calyx is tubular and its lobes, shorter than the calyx tube, are ovate and bent backwards. The club-shaped corolla is closed ('closed gentian'), deep blue in colour with white plicae and corolla lobes (turning purple or violet as it ages). It is three times as long as the calyx tube, up to 4cm (1⅝ in). The closed flowers usually serve to distinguish *G. andrewsii* from other closely related species. There is also a white form, *G. andrewsii* f. *albiflora* Britt., sometimes known as *G. andrewsii* var. *albiflora* (synonym: *G. flavida*). *G. clausa* Raf. is closely similar, but now ranked as a separate species. Dr Pringle subdivides the species into *G. andrewsii* and *G. andrewsii* var. *dakotica*. The latter is distinguished by having slightly enlarged corolla segments and by its occurrence in localities to the west of the range of *G. andrewsii*.

Despite its closed flowers this gentian is well worth a place in the garden. It is not difficult to cultivate, requiring only ordinary soil with some added peat. A situation in half shade is better than full sun. Sites in the rock garden are suitable, or alternatively it may be grown in half shade among other wild perennials.

Gentiana angulosa, see *G. verna* var. *angulosa*

Gentiana angustifolia Vill. (narrow-leaved gentian)

Found in the south-western Alps as far as Switzerland, and also in the Jura and Pyrenees. In the western Alps it replaces *G. clusii*, which is not found there. A lime-tolerant species, easily distinguishable by its long narrow leaves. It grows to a height of 5 to 10cm (2 to 4 in) with a rosette of hairless basal leaves. Stems with one or two pairs of leaves. The soft, dull-green rosette leaves are linear-lanceolate to lanceolate, 2 to 5.5cm (¾ to 2³⁄₁₆ in) in length and roughly three to five times as long as broad, having a breadth of only 5 to 9mm (³⁄₁₆ to ⅜ in). The leaf tips are blunt or only· shortly pointed. In this species the flowers are always borne on a stem, sometimes up to 7cm (2¾ in) tall. The calyx tube is bell shaped and measures over 12mm (½ in) in length; the lobes, which are shorter than half the length of the tube, are ovate-oblong. One character by which this species can be identified is the mode in which the calyx lobes stand out from the tube. The corolla is tubular to bell shaped; its lobes are ovate with long points, and the plicae are irregular and blunt. The flower is a vivid dark blue, though not so deep as those of *G. acaulis* and *G. clusii*. In the wild it flowers from May to August.

It is one of the best garden plants among the species of the *acaulis* group, and flowers quite profusely. It is a lime-lover and will tolerate moderate dryness, but in the garden will grow in soil of mildly acid reaction. If the garden soil is light, some loam should be added. Because of its long stems it makes good cut flowers.

Gentiana asclepiadea L. (willow gentian)

This species is widely distributed throughout southern and central Europe extending northwards as far as the Riesengebirge, the Carpathians and south-west Poland, southwards to central Italy, Corsica and central Greece, and eastwards into the north-west Ukraine, Asia Minor and the Caucasus. It is not a high alpine plant, but is found in the foothills and intermediate ranges, chiefly at altitudes of between 1,000 and 1,500m (3,300 and 5,000 ft), though occasionally as low as 500m (1,600 ft) or as high as 2000m (6,500 ft). This gorgeous, moisture-loving, lime-hating species grows mainly in open meadows, woodland clearings, moist hillsides, ravines and forest borders. In nature it is often associated with *Mentha longifolia*, *Origanum vulgare*, *Dryopteris filix-mas*, *Thelypteris phegopteris*, *Athyrium filix-femina*, *Veratrum album*, *Aconitum vulparia* and *Aruncus dioicus*. Similar communities look well in the wild garden.

This long-lived species is usually 50 to 60cm (18 in to 24 in) tall, though in favourable spots it may grow up to 1m (3 ft). It does not form basal rosettes, but its robust rootstock puts up vertical or overhanging stems with many pairs of leaves. The stems leaves are 5 to 8cm (2 to 3 long and 3.5cm (1⅜ in) broad; in shape they are ovate-lanceolate with long, tapering points and no leaf stalks. The numerous flowers are arranged on one side of the stem and are erect. They are 3.5 to 5cm (1⅜ to 2 in) in length and arise singly or in bunches of two to three from the upper leaf axils. The bell-shaped calyx is much shorter than the calyx tube. The corolla is bell shaped or club shaped, dark blue, spotted inside with purple and marked with pale, longitudinal stripes, sometimes white or light blue. The flower has five triangular lobes, with a blunt tooth in each of the folds.

Botanists have distinguished various forms, but these are of no significance to gardeners. Of greater importance are the distinct colour variants. Whereas the plants occurring in the Alps have flowers of moderately dark blue, the types found in southern Yugoslavia and in Albania are of a lighter and more brilliant blue. Seed from the Čakor Pass has been distributed by the writer to nurseries and enthusiasts, and this attractive type should soon become more widely known. Also much in demand is the albino form, *G. asclepiadea* 'Alba'. Purplish and pink forms are occasionally offered. Attempts to produce a colour scheme by growing *G. asclepiadea* from the Čakor Pass side by side with *G. a. 'Alba' and G. a.* 'Rosea' failed because the flowers did not open together but in the sequence given above.

It is true to say that the value of the willow gentian as a garden plant has not yet been fully recognised. During its flowering time from July to September it has few competitors for beds in half shade or for partly shaded areas in the larger rock garden. The flowers open in the mornings between 8 and 9 am and close between 5 and 6 pm. It prefers spots in half to full shade with constant moisture.

Suitable companions are small ferns, grasses and Turk's cap lilies. Solomon's seal makes a good partner, although it does not flower at the same time. An underplanting of alpine strawberries produces a charming effect, and when planted among dwarf rhododendrons the willow gentian, especially in its white flowering form, brings new life to these parts of the garden in late summer. As already mentioned, it is tolerant of differing soil reactions and will grow in the absence of lime. Other appropriate partners include small hostas and *Polygonum vacciniifolium*. It can be propagated by seed (the plants usually flower in their third year) or by dividing larger plants. Before being planted out, the plants should always be grown on in pots. Among other suitable companions for garden use are *Astrantia*, *Ranunculus aconitifolius*, ferns, grasses and sedges (*Luzula*, *Carex*). In the plant trials *G. asclepiadea* has been graded as a very valuable wild perennial, and *G. asclepiadea* 'Alba' as a valuable wild perennial.

Gentiana austromontana Pringle et Sharp

This species comes from a small area in western North America, chiefly from southern Virginia to north-eastern Tennessee and westwards to Carolina, growing at moderately high altitudes. Like *G. andrewsii*, it has closed flowers ('bottle gentian'). Its stems grow to a height of 30 to 45cm

(12 to 18 in) and carry ovate to lanceolate, glossy green leaves. The flowers on the upright stems appear over a long period throughout September and October. It is propagated by seed and can be grown in soil rich in humus with a mildly acid reaction in a place which is not too shady. It is described as one of the prettiest 'closed' gentians.

Gentiana autumnalis L.

SYNONYM: *G. porphyrio* J. F. Gmel.

A North American species from the Atlantic coast region from central New Jersey to southern Delaware and from south-western Virginia to South Carolina. It grows on moist, sandy meadows and in pinewoods. Each plant normally puts out two or three stems usually 40 to 50cm (14 to 20 in) high and unbranched. The leaves are linear or oblanceolate and single veined. The flowers are for the most part confined to the tops of the stems. The corolla is yellowish above and blueish below, but there are also blue, pink and white forms, the last being known as *G. a. f. albescens* (Fern.) Fern. It flowers from September to November.

A closely related species is *G. pennelliana* Fern. with five-veined petals; *G. autumnalis* has only three veins. It grows in west Florida where the mild climate allows it to flower from October to March.

In cultivation it prefers a light, sandy soil with plenty of moisture but good drainage. *G. autumnalis* is said to be one of the prettiest American species. Propagation is by seed.

Gentiana bavarica L. (Bavarian gentian)

Widely distributed throughout the Alps from the Maritime Alps as far as lower Austria, and also in the Abruzzi and Apennines. It extends from the subalpine to the high alpine zone where it colonises moist turf and pastures, fine screes kept moist by trickling water, spots irrigated by springs, and stream margins. This gentian tolerates a wide range of soil reactions, occurring both on limestone and primary rocks. Though often confused with the spring gentian (*G. verna*), it can be easily distinguished by the leaf shape.

Ranging in height from 4 to 20cm (1⅝ to 8 in) depending on the place where it grows, it forms small mats, green throughout the winter, which consist of erect angular non-flowering shoots 0.5 to 2cm (3⁄16 to ¾ in) tall. Among them are the terminal flowers, one to each shoot. The leaves are all of almost the same size (though the lower leaves are somewhat smaller), and are closely packed and overlapping. In shape they are rounded or blunt, spatulate or obovate, broadest in the lower third, 10 to 15mm (⅜ to ⅝ in) long, the width being barely half the length. There are no definite leaf rosettes, and on the stems there are three to four pairs of leaves.

The calyx is tubular to funnel shaped, 10 to 16mm (3/8 to 1/2 in) long, often with a tinge of violet; it may have narrow wings (1 to 2mm (1/32 to 1/16 in) wide), but there are sometimes none. The pointed, lanceolate calyx lobes are 5 to 6mm (1/4 in) long. The corolla is saucer shaped, roughly 2.5cm (1 in) long and 1.6 to 2cm (5/8 to 3/4 in) wide, deep-blue in colour, with a light-blue tube and five obtuse spreading lobes. Violet and white forms are occasionally found. In the wild it flowers from July till September.

This species has a close relative known as *G. rostanii* Reut. Some authors regard it as a form of *G. bavarica* and others as a species in its own right (see under *G. rostanii*). Another variant is *G. bavarica* var. *subacaulis* Schleicher, a low-growing plant with leaves which are almost circular and are closely set together like tiles on a roof. It is a high alpine form, occurring roughly between 2,400 and 3,000m (7,900 and 9,800 ft). This variety is notably floriferous. Other botanists divide the species into *G. b.* ssp. *bavarica* Tav. and *G. b.* ssp. *imbricata* Schleicher.

From the gardener's point of view *G. bavarica* is a tricky plant, much more difficult to keep than the spring gentian (*G. verna*). In the wild it grows in places where adequate moisture is always present. In the garden it likewise demands a moist place, though full sun is also essential. Limestone is not absolutely necessary; in the Alps the species also flourishes on soil derived from igneous rocks. In the garden it flowers in July and August. The only way of establishing a colony is to start with young plants raised from seed. The seed must be absolutely fresh. The best results are achieved by collecting seed from established plants and sowing it immediately. As soon as the seedlings are large enough to handle, prick them out into pots and in the following year plant them in their final positions without disturbing the root-balls. This advice on propagation by seed applies to related species as well. According to certain older writings, this gentian thrives in sandy soil from a bog mixed with chopped sphagnum. In warmer districts it often falls prey to aphids.

Gentiana bellidifolia Hook. f. (small New Zealand snow gentian)

A native of New Zealand, found on both the North and South Islands at altitudes from 600 to 1,800m (2,000 to 5,900 ft). It is a perennial with strong roots, differing in appearance depending on its habitat. It forms a basal rosette of leaves 10 to 15mm (3/8 to 5/8 in) long and 5 to 7mm (1/4 in) wide. Arising from the rosette are one to several stems 4 to 12cm (1 5/8 to

4¾ in) tall. The dark, brownish-green stem leaves are smaller than the basal leaves, always sessile and arranged in three to four pairs. The flowers, one to several (up to six) in number, are carried in dense, flat, terminal umbels which reach a height of 15 to 18cm (6 to 7 in). The calyx, (5/16 in) long, is half the length of the corolla and is deeply cut into narrow, pointed lobes. The bell-shaped flower is 15 to 18mm (⅝ to ¾ in) long and is also deeply cut. It has broad, blunt lobes, white in colour, sometimes marked with fine, purple veins, and often with greenish veins as well. The flowering time is June to July.

A high alpine variety from South Island is in circulation under the name *G. bellidifolia* var. *australis* Petric. It is a robust, low-growing form roughly 6 to 12cm (2⅜ to 4¾ in) in diameter with relatively large flowers (up to 2.5cm (1 in) in diameter).

Unfortunately, the nomenclature of the New Zealand gentians is somewhat confused. The species here described is similar to *G. saxosa* and like the latter is quite often seen in amateurs' collections. In cultivation this species likes a good, deep, lime-free soil with added peat in full sun, though the soil must never dry out. In cold districts winter protection is absolutely necessary and alpine-house cultivation may be preferable. It is propagated by seed, which should be as fresh as possible.

Gentiana bigelovii A. Gray

A gentian from the Rocky Mountains. Some authors refuse to accept it as a true species and regard it as a variety of *G. affinis*. It has robust purplish-green stems rising to a height of 30cm (12 in) or more with sessile flowers in the leaf axils. The flower colour is mid-blue and the flowering time is August. In some descriptions the flower colour is also given as whitish with a purple tinge. This species is the subject of serious confusion in seed exchanges, botanical gardens, etc. From *G. affinis* it is distinguished by the more spicate inflorescence (*G. affinis* forms more capitate clusters). In addition *G. bigelovii* has two ridges on the outside of the corolla lobes running down the upper part of the tube. It is not a plant of much garden value, and is of interest only to collectors and botanists. It requires full sun and well-drained soil, but otherwise presents no difficulties.

Gentiana bisetaea T. J. Howell

This species comes from Oregon, USA, where it grows in moist boggy places in the mountains near the coast. It is closely related to *G. calycosa*. *G. bisetaea* does not form basal leaf rosettes but puts up stems 25 to 45cm (10 to 18 in) tall carrying six to sixteen pairs of leaves, joined at the base into a sheath round the stem. The leaves are about 2.5cm (1 in) long, oval to oblong, though tending towards lanceolate near the top of the stem. They are thick in texture, rounded at the tips and narrowed at the base. The flowers appear in July to August and are bell shaped, and blue or purplish-blue in colour. It is distinguished from other closely related species by the lanceolate calyx lobes, which are about as long as the tube. Of interest only to collectors, it is easily grown in the garden in moist, lime-free soil.

Gentiana brachyphylla Vill. (short-leaved gentian)

SYNONYMS: *G. verna* L. var. *brachyphylla* Griseb., G. *verna* Bertoloni

This species occurs in the Alps (from the Maritime Alps as far as Styria and also in the Pyrenees and Transylvania. Very closely related to *G. verna*, *G. bavarica* and *G. favratii*, it is regarded by some authors as no more than a high alpine form of *G. verna*. It grows in the alpine and high alpine zones from 1,800 to 3,100m (5,900 to 10,000 ft), occasionally even higher. It is found chiefly in turf, but also on scree slopes and in snow hollows, preferring soils of low lime content.

It forms mats consisting of flowering and non-flowering shoots 3 to 6cm (1³⁄16 to 2³⁄8 in) high, or occasionally up to 15cm (6 in). All the leaves are basal, close set and overlapping like roof tiles, glossy, roughly of the same size about 1cm long and 0.5cm wide (¼ in long and ⅛ in wide), with a conspicuous cartilaginous margin with numerous papillae. Each flowering shoot carries only one saucer-shaped, deep azure-blue terminal flower, which is sessile or practically so. The calyx is half the length of the corolla. In the wild it blooms in July or August.

Though extremely difficult to grow in the open garden, it can be managed in the alpine house. The compost should contain an appropriate proportion of stone chippings; lime-free compost is advantageous, although the species sometimes occurs on limestone.

Flora Europaea divides *G. brachyphylla* into *G. b.* ssp. *brachyphylla* and *G. b.* ssp. *favratii*. The latter is listed in many publications as a species in its own right (*G. favratii* Rittener ex Favrat, *G. verna* var. *favratii* Rittener, *G. orbicularis* Schur). Some authors regard these plants as hybrids (*G. bavarica* × *G. verna*). Here we will follow *Flora Europaea*. The subspecies *favratii* differs from subspecies *brachyphylla* in the blunt, dark-green leaves, in the thin leaf margin and in the corolla lobes often broader than long. The flowers are deep blue, like those of *G. verna*. An important ecological difference is the fact that *G. brachyphylla* ssp. *favratii* always grows on limestone soils (Alps, Carpathians), usually at altitudes between 2,000 and 2,800m (6,500 and 9,200 ft).

This gentian is a better garden plant than *G. brachyphylla*. It prefers well-drained compost with an admixture of limestone rubble. Fresh seed germinates quickly. It is a tiny jewel for the enthusiastic grower of high alpines.

Gentiana bracteosa Greene

An American gentian from Colorado, it occasionally appears in seed lists but is often an impostor; the plants which grow from the seed are usually *G. septemfida* or similar species. The true species has no basal rosettes and puts up leafy stems about 30cm (12 in) tall. The leaves narrow markedly close to the stem. At the top of the stem the leaves are considerably larger, more ovate and embrace the lower part of the flowers like bracts. The funnel-shaped flowers are purplish-blue and open in August. It will grow best in deep, moderately moist soil in a site protected from burning sunshine.

Gentiana burseri Lapeyr

Pyrenees and south-western Alps. Closely related to *G. purpurea*. An erect plant, 60 to 90cm (2 to 3 ft) tall. The basal leaves are comparatively large, sometimes more than 23cm (9 in) long and roughly half that in breadth. The stem leaves become smaller towards the top. The flowers, arranged in whorls, arise from the axils of the leaves near the top of the stem. They are of a peculiar greenish-yellow, often dotted with brown spots. The corolla is about 4cm (1⅝ in) long. *Flora Europaea* divides the species into *G. b.* ssp. *burseri* and *G. b.* ssp. *villarsii* (Griseb.) Rouy. In the former the corolla lobes are acute, and in the latter they are blunt or only slightly pointed, and the flower is heavily marked with brown spots.

Not an attractive garden plant, and of interest only to collectors. Though it comes from limestone regions, it will grow without lime in the garden.

Gentiana cachemirica Decne.

Often spelt *G. cachemerica*. A Himalayan gentian from Kashmir and Pakistan, where it grows in rock fissures and on ledges at altitudes between 2,400 and 4,000m (7,900 and 13,000 ft), the flowering stems arching down from above. This gentian reaches a height of 8 to 15cm (3³⁄₁₆ to 6 in). The semi-erect, purple tinged shoots arise from a leaf rosette and carry a single, sessile, terminal flower, or occasionally a cluster of two or three flowers. In the wild it flowers from August to October. The basal leaves are ovate, and the stem leaves ovate or rounded, indistinctly three nerved and usually less than 1.2cm (½ in) long. The paired leaves are bluntly pointed and merge at the base into a short leaf stalk which surrounds the stem like a tube. The corolla, over 2.5cm (1 in) long, is bell shaped. In colour it is clear azure-blue with yellowish-white and blue stripes over 1cm (3⁄8 in) long. In the garden this gentian is often confused with *G. loderi*. The main differences are in the flowers. In *G. loderi* the calyx lobes are spoon shaped and recurved, the corolla is more tubular or bell shaped with large lobes and fringed, erect plicae. In contrast, *G. cachemirica* has linear, oblong calyx lobes, a bell-shaped corolla with narrow lobes, and plicae which have small lobes or are toothed.

An excellent garden plant. It likes well-drained, stony soil and is best grown in spots where the plant can hang down, such as the spaces in a dry-stone wall. It likes full sun. Unfortunately, the plant sold under this name is all too often not the genuine article, and the same is true of the seed exchanges. The description given by Oleg Polunin and Adam Stainton in their book *Flowers of the Himalaya* differs in certain respects from that given above. Propagation is by seed.

Gentiana calycosa Griseb.

Occurs in the western states of the USA, from California as far as British Columbia and eastwards into Alberta and Montana. Its main strongholds are in the southern Rocky Mountains. It grows there on rocky mountain sides and on mountain meadows near the treeline. It puts up numerous, more or less erect stems 15 to 40cm (6 to 14 in) long. These shoots carry the leaves in pairs, and at the top is a solitary flower (seldom more than one) without a stalk. The uppermost pair of leaves encircles the base of the flower. The leaves are broad ovate, or heart shaped, over 2.5cm (1 in) long, with three to five veins. The five calyx lobes are similar in shape to the leaves. The bell-shaped flowers appear in August–September; they are deep blue in colour with a pale throat and are 2.5 to 3.5cm (1 to 13⁄8 in) long.

This gentian is a worthwhile garden plant, easily cultivated. It likes full sun, although a little shade may be advantageous in the summer months. The soil should be moist, but stagnant water must not be allowed. It can be propagated by seed or by division in early spring.

In American publications it is sometimes found under the name *Pneumonanthe calycosa* (Griseb.) Greene.

Gentiana cephalantha French. ex Hemsl.

A gentian from Yunnan. It forms a much branched plant up to 45cm (18 in) tall. The flowers are arranged in clusters of six or more; they are

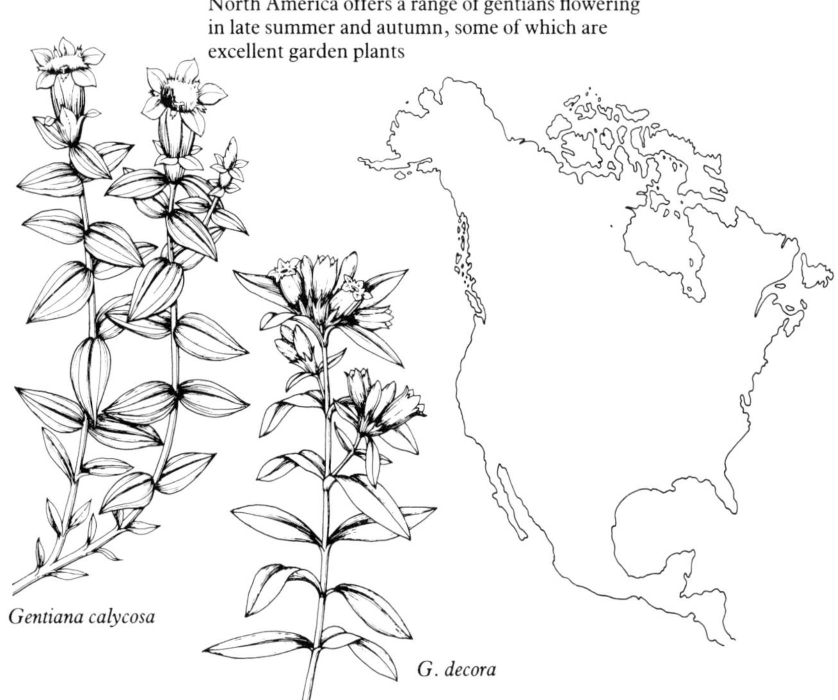

Figure 12 Gentians from North America

tubular, light blue, sometimes with darker veins. It flowers in August. In cultivation it is often confused with *G. rigescens*. In nature it grows on dry, stony mountain pastures. Seldom seen in gardens, it is not difficult provided it is given deep soil with good drainage.

Gentiana clausa Raf. (bottle gentian)

An American species found northwards as far as southern Maine and southern Quebec; extending westwards as far as north-eastern Tennessee and north-westwards to North Carolina. This species is very similar to *G. andrewsii* and has often been confused with it in the past. However, the two are easily distinguished: *G. andrewsii* has corolla lobes which are shorter and narrower than the broad, fringed plicae, while *G. clausa* has corolla lobes which are broader and longer than the plicae, which are cut into two or three segments. *G. clausa* is up to 50cm (20 in) tall. Its leaves are ovate to ovate-lanceolate, and glossy green. It is one of the 'closed' species, i.e. the flowers do not open fully. The flowering time extends from mid-August into October. The flowers are blue and are arranged in clusters at the tops of the stems; white forms are also known.

Despite its closed flowers it is an attractive garden plant, valuable because of its late flowering. Given a reasonably moist soil, it is suitable for sunny situations or for half shade. It looks well in large rock gardens, in the wild garden and at the margins of woodland. Propagation is by seed.

Gentiana clusii Perr. et Song. (trumpet gentian)

SYNONYMS: *G. acaulis* L.p.p., *Ericoila clusii* (Perr. et Song) A. D. Löve

Widely distributed throughout the central and eastern Alps, from Savoy to lower Austria, from Tessin to Croatia, the Jura, the Black Forest, the northern and eastern Carpathians and the Cevennes, where it grows in communities in hay meadows and poor pastures, on turf and rocks, usually at altitudes between 1,200 and 2,760m (3,900 to 9,000 ft), on limestone soils only. In nature its companions include *Ranunculus montanus*, *Primula farinosa*, *P. auricula*, *Buphthalmum salicifolium*, *Selaginella helvetica*, *Globularia cordifolia*, *Daphne cneorum*, *Draba aizoides*, *Thlaspi montanum*, *Dianthus gratianopolitanus*, *Saponaria ocymoides*, *Sedum dasyphyllum* and *Valeriana montana*. All these plants are available from general and alpine nurseries and make suitable partners for it in the garden.

G. clusii is easily distinguished from the other species of the *acaulis* group by the calyx lobes which are invariably pointed and never incised at the base, and by the fact that there are no green spots inside the flowers, but instead a dull-violet tinge. The rosettes are formed of stiff, leathery, glossy leaves, lanceolate or lanceolate-elliptic. The leaves are pointed, their greatest width being somewhat below the middle. The stem is short, 2 to 8cm (¾ to 3³⁄₁₆ in) long, though lengthening as the seed matures. It carries one or two pairs of small, ovate-lanceolate leaflets and a deep-blue (gentian-blue) flower, bell shaped to funnel shaped, often with a greenish tinge on the exterior. The calyx teeth, usually equal in length to the calyx, are pointed and pressed against the corolla. The flowering time extends from April into August, often with occasional late flowers in the autumn.

It is one of the most easily grown species of the *acaulis* group, and many garden strains have been derived from it. An ordinary, somewhat loamy soil which never becomes too dry will suit it well. It does not flower profusely unless given full sun. Despite numerous claims to the contrary, weak applications of fertiliser are beneficial.

Certain variants are of interest to gardeners, including *G. clusii* ssp. *undulatifolia* Beck, from the mountains surrounding the Italian lakes. The conspicuous undulations of the leaf edges persist in cultivation. *G. clusii* var. *costei* Brown-Blanquet (often listed as *G. costei*) is a variety with large flowers on long stalks derived from the south-western Alps. *G. clusii* also has numerous colour variants, namely white, reddish-purple, and even pink or yellowish.

Gentiana corymbifera T. Kirk (New Zealand snow gentian)

A native of New Zealand, it is found on the South Island, patchily distributed in the mountains of the interior from Marlborough–Nelson as far as Otaga. It is a plant of dry, grassy areas, found at moderate altitudes in spots with abundant rainfall; it invariably occurs in well-drained places near or upon moraines.

Arising from a stout rootstock is a robust more or less upright stem, 10 to 50cm (4 to 20 in) tall, depending on the location. At the base is a rosette of thick fleshy narrow leaves, 5 to 15cm (2 to 6 in) long and 1 to

Plate 7

This plate shows further species of Section Gentiana (syn. Section Coelanthe).

Above left: *Gentiana burseri* is closely related to *G. purpurea* but has yellow flowers. Grown in a favourable position it can reach up to 90cm (3 ft) in height, but in the wild some plants do not exceed 50cm (20 in). Though not a popular garden plant it is grown by enthusiasts.

Above right: A dense stand of yellow gentian (*G. lutea*) in an alpine meadow. This photograph was taken at the International Garden Exhibition in Munich in 1983, where the plants were grown under a successful simulation of natural conditions.

Below left: *G. punctata* is easily grown in the garden in deep, loamy soil. In nature it occurs both on limestone and on primitive rocks. The photograph shows it in the wild.

Below right: This plant, *G.* × *marcailhouana* (syn. *G.* × *burserlutea*) is a rare natural hybrid between *G. burseri* × *G. lutea*. The plant was photographed in the Botanical Garden in Munich/Nymphenburg where it was planted by the former curator, Wilhelm Schacht, who had previously found it in the Pyrenees.

2cm (3⁄8 to 3⁄4 in) broad. Up to the beginning of the inflorescence the stems are leafless, but from there upwards there are mostly paired leaves at the commencement of each bifurcation. The inflorescence is a corymb 5 to 15cm (2 to 6 in) in diameter. The numerous flowers, up to 1.8cm (3⁄4 in) in diameter, are white with faint purplish veins. The flowering time is August. Though often described as perennial, the plant is probably monocarpic, as it often dies after flowering.

Of all the New Zealand gentians this species is perhaps the most attractive for the garden. The stout, compact stem carrying numerous white flowers makes a striking contrast against the dark-green leaves. Its appearance is distinctive; there are no other species which might be confused with it. In the garden *G. corymbifera* requires full sun and good drainage, and the soil should be lime free. Propagation by seed presents no difficulties.

Gentiana cordifolia see *G. septemfida*

Plate 8

This plate shows a selection of gentians from Japan.

Above left: *Gentiana makinoi* comes from the mountains of central Japan and grows to a height of 30 to 60cm (12 to 24 in). Though not always a very striking plant, it nevertheless has a certain elegance.

Above right: *G. triflora* is an eastern-Asiatic species which is subject to wide morphological variation. Numerous varieties and forms are available. One of these forms is *G. triflora* var. *japonica* 'Royal Blue' which is grown for the cut-flower trade. The form shown here has more of its flowers in the terminal cluster.

Centre left: This pink gentian from Japan goes under the name *G. ishizuchii*, but its origin is not entirely clear.

Below left: *G. triflora* var. *japonica* (syn. *G. axillariflora*), a type from the island of Iturup.

Centre right: In Japan, *G. triflora* is an important garden plant of some commercial significance. This bunch was photographed in a Japanese florist's shop.

Below right: *G. scabra* var. *orientalis*, also photographed in a Japanese florist's, is grown on a commercial scale in Japan, especially as a pot plant.

Gentiana crassicaulis Duthie ex Burkhill

A species from China, occurring in damp patches in the mountains of West Szechuan and Yunnan. It has large basal leaves some 20cm (8 in) long, and leafy stems. The flowers, which appear in August, are greenish-white and are carried in close clusters at the tops of the stems, though usually hidden by the topmost pairs of leaves. An easily grown plant, given full sun and good drainage it will produce abundant seed. However, it is of little garden value and of interest mainly to collectors.

Gentiana cruciata L. (cross gentian)

This widely distributed species is found in southern, central and eastern Europe, western Siberia, the Caucasus, Armenia, Asia Minor and Iran. Despite this wide distribution it is nowhere very common. It grows in short grass on dry meadows and pastures, on sunny slopes covered by shrubs, and at forest margins. It is found at all altitudes up to 1,500m (5,000 ft), and occasionally even higher. It generally prefers limey soils.

It forms a basal leaf rosette which is renewed every year. From it arise several thick, erect, leafy stems, usually unbranched, sometimes having a violet tinge. The stem leaves are lanceolate and are arranged in pairs, each pair being placed crosswise to the next; they usually have three (occasionally five) nerves. The flowers, normally with four corolla lobes, are carried in terminal or axillary clusters. The corolla is club shaped or bell shaped, erect, externally dirty-blue or greenish, internally sky-blue, about 2 to 2.5cm (¾ to 1 in) in length. Flowering time is July to October. The plant varies greatly in overall height, from 10 to 50cm (4 to 20 in), though in the garden it is usually about 40cm (16 in) tall. *Flora Europaea* distinguishes *G. cruciata* ssp. *cruciata* and *G. cruciata* ssp. *phlogifolia* (Schott et Kotschy) Tutin (the Transylvanian gentian). The latter is listed in certain older publications as a species in its own right (*G. phlogifolia* Schott et Kotschy). The following points distinguish it from *G. cruciata* ssp. *cruciata*: calyx lobes broad triangular, usually shorter than the tube; corolla three times as long as the calyx. *G. cruciata* ssp. *phlogifolia*: calyx lobes narrower, linear to linear-lanceolate, longer than the tube; corolla twice as long as the calyx. In cultivation these subspecies have been confused with one another and also with other closely related species. Attempts to select strains of better flower colour might be worthwhile.

This is not a gentian which will attract crowds of admirers, yet it deserves a place in the garden. Easily grown, it prefers dryish soil in full sun and is well suited for large rock gardens (flowering at a time when colour is scarce) or for planting in front of shrubs (forest margin communities). It can be propagated by seed or division. Ideal companions are *Inula ensifolia* 'Compacta' and *Festuca ovina*.

Gentiana dahurica Fisch.

Asia Minor to north-west China. It forms a strong rootstock, its collar covered with fibres. The stems are upright or slightly sloping, 30 to 40cm (12 to 16 in) tall. The basal leaves are lanceolate, up to 20cm (8 in) long, with one to three veins. The stem leaves are narrower and shorter. The narrow tubular flowers, about 3cm (1¼ in) long, with four, pointed corolla lobes, are pale to deep blue with white spots. They are carried singly or in small clusters in the upper leaf axils and appear in August.

It will grow in full sun in any deep garden soil, with or without lime. It is propagated by seed, though the seed and plants offered are often not true; usually they are forms of *G. gracilipes*, *G. cruciata*, *G. cruciata* ssp. *phlogifolia*, *G. decumbens* and others. Suitable associates include *Adenophora* species, *Geranium nodosum* and *Polygonatum falcatum*.

Gentiana decora Pollard

A little-known North American species which grows in woods from Georgia to Virginia. It reaches a height of 20 to 25cm (8 to 10 in) and its leaves are lanceolate-elliptic to ovate-elliptic. The stems, usually unbranched, have terminal clusters of tubular white flowers with blue or violet markings in the interior; it flowers in autumn.

Gentiana decumbens L.f. (Siberian gentian)

This species extends from eastern Russia through Siberia into Mongolia and southwards to the Himalaya where it grows at considerable altitudes. It favours well-drained spots with adequate moisture during the growing period. It forms a distinct rosette of narrow leaves 7 to 8cm (2¾ to 3³⁄₁₆ in) long and only 1.2cm (½ in) broad. The stems which arise from the rosette are 25 to 30cm (10 to 12 in) long; more or less prostrate at first, they ascend at the tips. They bear two or three pairs of stem leaves, 3.5 to 4cm (about 1½ in) long, oblong or narrow-oblong, their bases surrounding the stem. The flowers, sessile or on short stalks, are borne in clusters of two or three at the ends of the stems or in the axils of the upper leaves. They are bell shaped, about 3cm (1³⁄₁₆ in) long, and have rounded or ovate lobes much longer than the plicae. In colour they are a fine, middle blue, though deep blue to purple-blue forms are also seen. The flowering time is August. In cultivation this species presents no problems and is an excellent plant for rock gardens or similar situations. It grows in stony, well-drained soil in full sun.

There is some confusion as to its correct identity, many other species and hybrids hiding under the name *G. decumbens*. The species can be distinguished from its close relatives as follows: *G. olivieri* has an undivided calyx tube; *G. gracilipes* has longer flower pedicels, and its flowers are longer and more tubular; *G. straminea* has yellowish flowers; *G. dahurica* has a shorter calyx tube and narrower flowers.

Gentiana dendrologii Marq.

A native of Western China. The stems, about 35cm (14 in) long, are upright or ascending. Basal leaves lanceolate to linear, up to 25cm (10 in) long; stem leaves broader, up to 10cm (4 in) long. The flowers are carried in clusters at the ends of the stems or in the upper leaf axils. Calyx 1.5cm (⅝ in) long, corolla white, cylindrical, 3.5 to 4cm (1⅜ to 1⅝ in) long. The seed offered is not always true. Of interest mainly to collectors.

Gentiana depressa D. Don

A native of the Himalayas, found chiefly in Nepal, Sikkim and south-eastern Tibet. Not very common. Chiefly at altitudes of 3,300 to 4,300m (10,800 to 14,100 ft). A low, tufted plant with spreading stems. The leaves on the non-flowering stems are narrow; those on the flowering stems are broad-ovate, overlapping and surrounding the stem. The basal rosettes are lax and measure up to 2cm (¾ in) in diameter. The flowers are terminal, pale blue or greenish blue and broad, bell shaped with triangular corolla lobes roughly equal in length and breadth. The corolla is 2 to 3cm (¾ to 1³⁄₁₆ in) long, with greenish-white stripes, speckled with purplish-blue externally and purple internally. The tubular calyx has oval, pointed, erect, white edged lobes about 6mm (¼ in) long.

This is a beautiful and unmistakable plant which presents a challenge to the experienced grower. Despite the high altitude from which it comes it is not fully hardy and is not yet widely grown. It flowers in late summer, in the wild not until September–November. In the garden it prefers an exposed, sunny place with heavy stony soil and good drainage. Its seeds usually fail to ripen and this mode of propagation is therefore uncertain, but as it suckers so readily vegetative propagation is simple. It is perhaps best grown in pots in an alpine house.

Gentiana dinarica G. Beck.

A plant of limestone districts in the mountains of south-western Yugoslavia, Albania and the Abruzzi. It is a member of the *acaulis* group with stiff, broad elliptic, bright-green rosette leaves. The plant reaches a height of up to 7cm (2¾ in). The calyx lobes are more than half as long as the tube, narrow lanceolate and constricted at the base. The flower is tubular bell-shaped and of a superb blue colour; it has no greenish spots or flecks in the throat. The flowering time is June.

In the garden this gorgeous gentian produces its flowers in abundance over a long period. Its flowers are large in comparison with the other parts of the plant. It requires full sun and loamy soil containing lime, with adequate moisture during the growing period. It can be propagated by division or seed. Some nurseries offer a particularly vigorous type under the name *G. dinarica* 'Frohnleiten'. Another variety is *G. dinarica* 'Härlen' with narrower leaves and pale-blue trumpets on stems about 10cm (4 in) high. In plant trials the species has been classed as a perennial for enthusiasts.

Gentiana divisa (Kirk) Cheesem. (snowball gentian)

This species is a native of the South Island of New Zealand, where it occurs in high mountain terrain southwards from southern Nelson, at altitudes of 900 to 1,900m (3,000 to 6,250 ft). It grows on patches of grass and other perennials and among shrub vegetation on cold, wind-swept spots between patches of melting snow. It is a robust, firmly rooted perennial of unmistakable appearance. Its broad, rounded, sometimes reddish leaves form an overlapping rosette from which arise numerous much branched stems 5 to 20cm (2 to 8 in) long. They carry terminal clusters of rounded flowers, sometimes so densely packed that the leaves are almost hidden. Against the dark, stony background of the mountains they often resemble snowballs (hence the name). Another variety is *G. divisa* var. *magnifica* (Kirk) Allan, which unlike the species has only a few stem leaves or none at all.

One of the less well-known New Zealand gentians, this species is certainly worthy of a trial, though it remains to be seen whether it will prosper in our gardens.

Gentiana dijlgensis see *G. pyrenaica*

Gentiana elwesii C. B. Clarke

A little-known Himalayan species found mainly in Sikkim at altitudes above 4,000m (13,100 ft). It has sometimes been described as annual, though other authors speak of it as perennial. It forms large rosettes of elliptical to ovate leaves approximately 5cm (2 in) long. The stem leaves are shorter and wider. The flowers are carried in terminal clusters; calyx

1cm (3⁄8 in) long, calyx teeth unequal, corolla tubular and pale blue, closed at the apex, 3cm (1 3⁄16 in) long. Flowers in August. The whole plant is some 30cm (12 in) tall. For collectors only. Plants bearing this name are often impostors.

Gentiana farreri Balf. f.

Discovered in 1914 by Farrer and Purdom and introduced not long afterwards. Grows in high, alpine turf from north-western Kansu to Tibet. The discovery of this gentian and its flowering in Edinburgh in 1916 were a minor sensation. As a young plant it forms a small rosette of linear leaves. This rosette then puts out branching shoots 10 to 15cm (4 to 6 in) long clothed with several pairs of leaves. Each leaf joins its opposite to form a short tube around the stem. The bright-green leaves are long and narrow, some 3.5cm (1 3⁄8 in) in length and distinctly recurved. The solitary tubular flowers at the ends of the shoots are 6–7cm (2 3⁄8 to 2 3⁄4 in) long and at its best are brilliant pale-blue in colour, generally described as Cambridge blue, though varying considerably in its native China. When open the flowers have a diameter of some 3cm (1 3⁄16 in). The throat is white, and the external surface striped with yellowish-white. Flowering time is late summer. *G. farreri* is distinguished from the other species of autumn-flowering Asiatic gentians by its characteristic narrow leaves.

G. farreri is a garden treasure, and though like its relatives it prefers lime-free soil, it is nevertheless much more tolerant of lime. It needs an open spot with good drainage but adequate moisture during the growing period. On the whole it is not difficult in cultivation. It sets seed freely and can easily be propagated in this way. It can also be increased by cuttings taken in late July or in August, and vigorous plants can be divided in March. In gardens where other Asiatic gentians are grown, vegetative propagation is advisable, as the species hybridises readily (see under Gentian Hybrids). Doubts have been raised whether the plants nowadays offered under the name *G. farreri* still represent the true and unadulterated species yet a recent re-introduction will dispel such doubt. In plant trials it has been classified as a collectors item.

Gentiana fetisowii Regel et C. Winkl.

A native of Western Siberia, East Turkestan and north-eastern China. It forms a long-leafed rosette from which arises a solitary flower stem 20 to 30cm (8 to 12 in) and sometimes over 40cm (16 in) tall. The lanceolate basal leaves are 15cm (6 in) long or even more, while the stem leaves are smaller and arranged in pairs crosswise to one another. The flowers are carried in clusters at the top of the stem or in the axils of the upper leaves. The tubular or bell-shaped corolla is two to three times longer than the calyx; its recurved spreading lobes are ovate and pointed at the tips. The flower is purplish-blue to deep blue, with brownish spots in the interior of the tube. Flowering time is August.

This species is closely related to *G. decumbens*. Both have a split calyx, the differences between them being as follows: *G. fetisowii* normally puts up only one flowering stem, the corolla is tubular bell shaped, the flowers form a bushy cluster and the overy is unstalked. *G. decumbens* has several flowering stems, the corolla is widely bell shaped, the flowers are arranged more in the form of a raceme and the ovary is stalked.

Cultivation presents no difficulties, but for the ordinary gardener *G. decumbens* or a similar species such as *G. gracilipes* is preferable. *G. fetisowii* is really a plant for collectors. It is propagated by seed, but all kinds of other species masquerade among the plants and seeds offered under its name.

Gentiana fischeri P. Smirnov

Central Asia and the Altai mountains at 1,800m (5,900 ft). Seed under this name has recently been distributed through the seed exchanges. There is some doubt as to the name. In the bulletin of the Moscow Natural History Society (1937) the valid name was stated to be *G. gebleri* Fisch. ex Bunge, but in other references *G. gebleri* is put under *G. septemfida*. However, it seems certain that *G. fischeri* P. Smirnov belongs to the same category as *G. septemfida*. Further information will emerge as it becomes better known in cultivation.

Gentiana freyniana Bornm.

Found at high altitudes in Asia Minor. In the garden often confused with *G. septemfida*. The rootstock puts up erect, leafy shoots. At the base of the stem the leaves are scale-like, but higher up they are in pairs united in a tube round the stem; they are 2.5cm (1 in) long, linear-lanceolate with rather blunt points. Usually they have three veins. The plant is 15 to 30cm (6 to 12 in) tall, usually with a single flower at the top of each shoot; when there are two or three flowers they are stalkless. The calyx lobes are linear. The corolla is club shaped with an open mouth, bright blue to purplish-blue. Flowering time is August to September.

Though often confused with *G. septemfida*, this species can be distinguished by its plicae, which are bifid and not fimbriate or many cleft as in *G. septemfida*. The two species cross readily. For this reason it is safer to propagate them by cuttings. Because of its long flowering season—often of many weeks' duration—it is a valuable plant for the rock garden. Ordinary garden soil and full sun meet its requirements.

Gentiana frigida Haenke, Styrian gentian

Found in the Styrian Alps, Carpathians, Tatra and south-western Bulgaria. It grows on stony turf and rocks at altitudes of 2,000 to 2,400m (6,500 to 7,900 ft), always on lime-free soils. Uncommon in the eastern Alps, its main occurrence is in the Carpathians. Some botanists regard it as a geographical race of *G. algida*, a species found in Asia and North America.

A perennial species, upright or spreading, 5 to 15cm (2 to 6 in) tall. Stems unbranched, basal leaves narrow spathulate, up to 7.5cm (3 in) long. The pale-green stem leaves are thick in texture and tend to form a sheath at the base. The flowers, solitary or two or three in number, are carried at the ends of the shoots and are divided into five segments. The erect, membranous, bell-shaped calyx has five ovate-lanceolate lobes. The bell-shaped corolla is yellowish, flecked and striped with blue. Flowering time is July–September.

Not an easy garden plant, though sometimes grown by enthusiasts and connoisseurs. It should be planted in stony soil derived from igneous rock, with a top dressing of granite chippings or similar stone. Closely related to *G. algida* (*G. algida* var. *nubigena*). Another similar species is *G. przewalskii*.

Gentiana froelichii Jan. (Karawanken gentian)

Grows in the Austrian Alps and Karawanken from 1,800 to 2,400m (6,000 to 7,800 ft), occasionally lower, invariably in a humus-rich soil over a limestone base. It is found on rocks and screes in the dwarf-pine zone. In the wild its associates are *Campanula zoysii*, *Primula wulfeniana*, *Carex firma*, *Saxifraga squarrosa*, *S. crustata*, *Dryas octopetala*, *Helianthemum oelandicum* ssp. *alpestre* and *Rhodothamnus chamaecistus*.

G. freyniana forms lax, leafy rosettes from which arise spreading stems 3cm (1³⁄16 in) tall, each carrying a single terminal flower. Each stem has one or two pairs of leaves which tend to sheath the base of the stem. The calyx is green, tubular-bell shaped and surrounded by the uppermost pair of leaves. The calyx teeth are pointed and lanceolate, somewhat shorter than the calyx tube. The corolla is funnel shaped, watery blue to sky-blue, unspotted. Flowering time July–August.

This species is somewhat difficult in cultivation and dislikes any form of root disturbance. Young plants should be carefully established without breaking their root-balls. It requires full sun, soil with plenty of limestone rubble, and good drainage in winter. A plant for the expert.

Gentiana gelida Bieb.

A native of the Caucasus, Asia Minor and Iran, this species does not form basal rosettes but puts up semi-erect leafy stems 30 to 35cm (12 to 14 in) tall. At the base of the stems the leaves are scale-like, but upwards they increase in size. The flowers are bell shaped, pale yellow, appearing in July or August. Closely related to *G. septemfida* and *G. freyniana*, this species is easily distinguished by its flower colour. In the garden it associates happily with *G. septemfida*, requiring full sun and good garden soil like the latter. Propagated by seed, though germination is undependable, and also by cuttings.

Gentiana georgei Diels

First collected by Forrest on the eastern slopes of the Lichiang range, where it grows on open mountain meadows at altitudes of around 4,000m (13,100 ft). It forms a basal rosette of narrow, sharply pointed leaves 6.5cm (3 in) long and 1.25cm (½ in) broad. The largest leaves on the flowering stem are up to 4cm (1⅝ in) long, tinged with purple, with roughish margins. The stems, some 15cm (6 in) tall, carry a single terminal flower. The corolla is bell shaped, over 5cm (2 in) long. In colour it varies from deep purple-blue to deep clear-blue; the exterior is striped green, the interior spotted at the base. It flowers in autumn. A rare but attractive species which requires stony soil rich in humus. Seed germination is very poor and it is doubtful whether this species is in cultivation at present.

Gentiana gilvostriata Marquand

Found by Kingdon Ward in Upper Burma near the Tibetan frontier, where it grows in open stony places among rhododendrons on lime-free soil. It forms small, tufted spreading mats of leaf rosettes only 2 to 5cm (¾ to 2 in) tall. The short flower stems carry sky-blue flowers with darker bands on the exterior; the interior is paler with deeper spots. Flowering in August, it is a beautiful and unmistakable species, unfortunately not widely distributed. Not too difficult in the garden; provided it is given a sunny position in well-drained peaty soil, it is entirely hardy. It is propagated by seed or by cuttings from the basal shoots.

Gentiana glauca Pallas

SYNONYM: *G. glauca* var. *major* Ledeb.

This species grows on alpine pastures in the southern Rocky Mountains, and also in Siberia, Kamtschatka, Alaska and Japan. If forms narrow leaf rosettes with small non-flowering shoots resembling stolons. The flowering rosettes have leaves only 1.2cm (½ in) long, rounded-ovate or spoon shaped, three veined, thick and grey-green in colour. These rosettes put up erect flowering stems some 10cm (4 in) tall, bearing three or four pairs of stem leaves. At the top are one to three flowers, and in the axils of the topmost leaves there is usually a single flower, which, unlike the terminal flowers, has a stalk. The flowers are between 1.2 and 1.8cm (½ and ¾ in) in diameter, are blue or pale blue with a white interior, though there are different types, as might be expected from the wide distribution of the plant. The flowering season is June to August.

Seldom seen in cultivation, it requires well-drained, sandy soil in the coolest possible place.

Gentiana gracilipes Turrill

A native of Kansu in China. This well-known species, widely grown in gardens, is often confused with other species and sometimes incorrectly named *G. purdomii*. It forms a central rosette of narrow leaves about 15cm (6 in) long and up to 1.5cm (⅝ in) wide, dark green on the upper side and pale green on the under side. The neck of the root is covered with tufts of fibres. Arising from the rosette are three or four lax flowering stems with pairs of leaves. The stems are branched, and at the ends of the branches are the solitary flowers on very long 5cm (2 in) stalks. The corolla is narrowly bell shaped and deep purplish-blue within, greenish without, roughly 3 to 4cm (1³⁄₁₆ to 1⅝ in) long and 1.3cm (½ in) in diameter. The corolla lobes are ovate-triangular. In general appearance it resembles *G. dahurica*, but can be distinguished by the split calyx which differs from the tubular calyx of *G. dahurica*.

A pretty species which grows in any ordinary garden soil. It is propagated by seed, which sets abundantly. There are certain plants widely grown in gardens under the name *G. purdomii*. All such plants belong to section *aperta* and in most instances they are really *G. gracilipes*.

Gentiana grombczewskii Kusn.

Often misspelt in the English literature as *G. grombezewikii* or *G. grombezewskii*. A native of Eastern Turkestan. A lax, tufted perennial up to 40cm (16 in) tall with upright or spreading stems. The oblong-lanceolate basal leaves are up to 30cm (12 in) long and five-veined; the stem leaves are up to 10cm (4 in) long. The tubular, funnel-shaped, yellow flowers are borne in terminal clusters. Flowering time is August. Easily cultivated but of little garden value, it is a plant for collectors.

Gentiana hexaphylla Maxim.

A native of Eastern Tibet and Kansu. A pretty plant with certain distinctive characteristics, the chief of which is that the parts of the flower are in sixes, as opposed to related species in which the parts are in fives; the botanical name refers to this point. It does not form a central rosette, but is a bushy plant with numerous stems some 15cm (6 in) long; when out of flower it sometimes resembles one of the mossy saxifrages. The leaves are small, linear, usually not more than 1.2cm (½ in) long, and arranged in whorls of six around the stem. At the end of the shoot there is a close whorl of leaves which surrounds the calyx. The flowers are solitary and terminal. The calyx lobes (six in number) and tube are of roughly equal length. The tubular flower is 3.5 to 4cm (1⅜ to 1⅝ in) long and 1.5cm (⅝ in) in diameter when fully open; the six corolla lobes have pointed tips. The flower is pale blue to water blue with six, broad, blue bands on the exterior and greenish markings in the interior. Flowering begins at the end of July and reaches its peak in August. One well-known hybrid of this species is *G.* × *hexa-farreri* (see Gentian Hybrids).

Given moist, lime-free soil and full sun, the plant is not difficult to grow. It can be propagated by seed, division or cuttings. After two years in the same place the plants tend to deteriorate. When divided and replanted in fresh soil the pieces will grow with renewed vigour.

Gentiana jamesii Hemsley

SYNONYMS: *G. nipponica* var. *kawakamii* Makino, *G. kawakamii* (Makino) Makino

This pretty gentian comes from Japan, the Kurile Islands and Korea. Not widely distributed in gardens, it is sometimes grown under the Japanese name Rishiririndo. Sometimes only 5cm (2 in) tall, its angulated stems, often tinged purplish red, sometimes rise to 21cm (8¼ in). The leaves are broad lanceolate or elongated with a whitish margin. The flowers form a narrow tube of purplish-blue colour, appearing from July to September. A half shady position in moist soil suits it well, though good drainage is necessary. It is propagated by seed, though this is seldom obtainable. There is a somewhat larger type with flowers 2.2 to

3cm (7/8 to 1 3/16 in) long and a thicker corolla. It comes from moister places and is known as *G. jamesii* var. *robusta* (Hara) Ohwi (syn. *G. nipponica* var. *robusta* Hara).

Gentiana jesoana Nakai see *G. triflora* var. *japonica* (Kusn.) Hara

Gentiana kurroo Royle

Found in north-western China, Pakistan and Kashmir at altitudes from 1,800 to 2,700m (5,900 to 8,800 ft). Many of the plants circulating under this name are not the genuine article. The true species is a pretty plant with a well-developed rosette. The rosette leaves are linear to lanceolate, up to 10cm (4 in) long and pointed. Springing from the basal rosette are the stems, 5 to 15cm (2 to 6 in) or occasionally up to 25cm (10 in) tall. They are prostrate at first but then ascend at their tips. At the tops of the stems and also in the axils of the upper stem leaves are the large, usually solitary flowers, pure blue in colour with greenish spots and whitish tints in the interior. They are narrow, bell shaped or funnel shaped, though they open widely at the mouth. The calyx tube is entire, 1.2cm (½ in) long and has sharply pointed lobes roughly the same length as the tube. As the plant flowers late in the year, from September to October, seeds often fail to ripen well in the garden.

The true plant is well worth a place in any garden. It needs stony soil with perfect drainage, and should preferably be given protection from winter wet. Doubt has been cast on its hardiness. It is propagated by seed.

Gentiana lagodechiana see *G. septemfida*

Gentiana lawrencei Burkhill

A native of Siberia, first collected in the Lake Baikal district. A rather feeble plant, lacking the good constitution of related species, it often dies after a year or two. The basal rosette puts out shoots and stolons up to 15cm (6 in) long carrying pairs of leaves over 2.5cm (1 in) in length. At the end of each shoot is a solitary flower of turquoise blue colour, somewhat paler inside, with broad, dark bands of blue on the outside. In appearance it closely resembles *G. farreri* and will cross with it.

A beautiful but delicate species. It requires perfect drainage in stony soil and full sun. Unfortunately it seldom sets seed.

Gentiana ligustica R. de Vilmorin et Chopinet

Found on limestone soils in the Maritime Alps and Central Appennines, this species belongs to the *acaulis* group. The leaves are oblong-obovate to broadly ovate, at most three times as long as wide. The calyx teeth are less than half as long as the tube, broadly ovate, narrowed at the base. The corolla has green spots in the throat; its lobes are sharply pointed. Though it can be grown without much difficulty given an open site with adequate soil moisture, it is not often seen in gardens.

Gentiana linearis Froel.

An American species of sparse occurrence in Canada and many states of the USA, it is found in moist places. It is a robust plant 30 to 70cm (12 in to 2 ft 4 in) tall. The linear-oblong leaves are 4 to 9cm (1⅝ to 4½ in) long and up to 1cm (⅜ in) wide and are arranged in pairs on the stems. The flowers, usually two to four in number, are carried in terminal clusters and also singly in the axils of the upper leaves. The corolla is tubular, 3 to 4cm (2⅛ to 2⅝ in) long and blue or white in colour. In nature it flowers in July to September and in cultivation never before late summer. In the garden it demands a very moist spot, and the soil must be acid with a high content of peat. Propagation is by seed.

Gentiana loderi Hook.

This species is found in Kashmir at altitudes of around 3,000m (9,800 ft). A neat-growing plant, its weak stems, 10 to 15cm (4 to 6 in) long, prostrate at first but ascending at the tips, carry a solitary stalkless flower. The corolla is tubular-bell shaped and clear blue in colour. The paired leaves are broadly elliptic with rounded tips, sessile or shortly stalked, some 12mm (½ in) in length and nearly as much in breadth, with three veins and of comparatively thick texture.

A beautiful plant and well worth growing in the garden. The flowers are of striking colour and contrast well against the leaves. The flowering time is July–August. Unfortunately the plants offered are often not true; it is often confused with *G. cachemirica*, though this species has linear oblong calyx lobes in contrast to the spoon-shaped lobes of *G. loderi*. It is not as easy to grow as some gentians, and requires gravelly, lime-free soil in full sun.

Gentiana lowndesii Blatter

A Himalayan species very close to *G. kurroo*. The calyx lobes are shorter than the calyx tube, and the corolla lobes are longer than broad.

Gentiana lutea L. (yellow gentian)

Found in Portugal and northern Spain, Italy, the Cevennes, the Alps and their foothills, northwards as far as central France and southern Germany, the Carpathians, the Balkans, northern and western Anatolia. Sometimes sparsely scattered but usually gregarious on the grassy floors of mountain corries, in unmanured hay meadows, on scree slopes, pastures, rocks, in grassland and fens. Mainly in the alpine zone, ascending up to 2,500m (8,200 ft), on lime-containing soils. In some districts it has become scarce from the depredations of those who dig up its roots for medicinal use.

An imposing plant from 50 to 190cm (20 in to 6 ft) tall, devoid of hairs. The tap root may be as thick as a man's arm and has few branches. The bluish-green, elliptical leaves have conspicuous ribs five to seven in number. They are up to 30cm (12 in) long and 15cm (6 in) wide, the lower leaves having short stalks while the upper leaves are sessile. The flowers are carried in clusters of three to ten in the leaf axils, and are golden yellow in colour with a short tube. The corolla lobes are oblong-linear and pointed, and spread out in the shape of a star. In the wild it is associated with many other plants, some of which can be grown beside it in the garden, such as *Thalictrum aquilegifolium*, *Dianthus superbus*, *Arabis alpina*, *Aconitum napellus* and *A. vulparia*, *Rosa alpina*, *Thymus serpyllum*, *Myosotis alpestris*, *Scabiosa lucida*, *Valeriana montana*, *Campanula scheuchzeri*, *Achillea erba-rotta*, *Doronicum spp.*, *Carlina acaulis*, *Erigeron alpinus*, *Gentiana punctata*, *G. asclepiadea*, *Juniperus nana*, *Crocus albiflorus*, *Alchemilla vulgaris*, *Aster bellidiastrum*, *Daphne mezereum*, *Athyrium filix-femina*, *A. distentifolium*, *Digitalis grandiflora*, *Lilium martagon*, *Veronica fruticans*, *Campanula cochlearifolia* and *Molinia caerulea*.

This gentian demands patience on the part of the gardener. Young plants should be raised in pots and planted out. However, many years will pass before they attain their full stature. It is at home in sunny places in the wild garden or the larger rock garden, though it can be used as a feature plant elsewhere. A sun-lover, *G. lutea* is not fussy about soil, but good drainage is essential. It is propagated by seed, as the thick tap roots are unsuitable for division.

Botanists distinguish *G. lutea* ssp. *lutea* with free anthers from *G. lutea* ssp. *symphandra* (Murb.) Hayek, with anthers joined into a tube. The latter grows only in the south-eastern Alps and the Balkans.

Gentiana macrophylla Pall.

This species, a native of Siberia, Mongolia and northern China, is a strong-growing plant with basal leaves over 30cm (12 in) long (hence the name *macrophylla*), though in cultivation they are somewhat smaller 20cm (8 in). In shape they are lanceolate to oblong with roughish margins and three or sometimes five veins. The basal leaves do not form a definite rosette. The upright stems are 30 to 45cm (12 to 18 in) tall and have long internodes. The stem leaves are smaller than the basal leaves. The pale-blue, tubular flowers, 2.5cm (1 in) long, are borne in small numbers in the upper leaf axils and in a terminal raceme. The flowering time is August–September. An unattractive plant of little garden value.

Gentiana makinoi Kusn.

A native of the mountains of central Japan. An erect-growing species without rosettes sending up leafy shoots to heights of 30 to 60cm (12 to 24 in). The ends of the stems carry several flowers and there are also flowers in the axils of the upper leaves. The stem leaves are lanceolate to oval, 5cm (2 in) long, with three veins; the uppermost leaves are the largest and have conspicuous points. The calyx tube is 12mm (½ in) long and is entire; the calyx lobes are unequal in length: two of them are usually long and linear with sharp points, while the other three are shorter and almost triangular. The flowers are 3.5 to 4cm (1⅜ to 1⅝ in) long and tubular-bell shaped. In colour they are pale blue with irregular spots. There are types with flowers of darker blue in which the spotting is inconspicuous. The flowering time extends from August to September. There are also white-flowered forms. Propagation is by seed.

Though by no means well known, it is not without a certain elegance and has recently appeared in increasing numbers in gardens. Though described as hardy, it is advisable to give the plants some protection against severe frost. In cultivation it is not difficult, provided it can be given lime-free soil. Places in full sun should be avoided; it prefers half shade.

Gentiana menziesii see *G. sceptrum*

Gentiana newberryi A. Gray

An unmistakable species from the mountains of California (Sierra Nevada), southern Oregon and Nevada, where it grows at altitudes of up to 3,000m (9,800 ft). A dwarf plant, 5 to 10cm (2 to 4 in) in height, which forms mats of short shoots some 5cm (2 in) long from which the flowering stems arise. The leaves of the basal rosettes are obovate or spathulate and some 2.5cm (1 in) long. The obovate or lanceolate stem leaves are carried in pairs and are about 1.2cm (½ in) long. The stalkless flowers are borne at the end of the stems, solitary or occasionally in twos. The calyx is tubular and somewhat longer than the lanceolate calyx lobes. The corolla is pale blue and has five broad, brownish bands on the exterior surface; in the interior it is white with greenish spots. The calyx lobes are oval and sharply pointed, longer than the plicae. The flowering time extends from summer to autumn.

This species is easily distinguished from all other American gentians, notably by its mat-forming tendency and the short flowering stems. The flower can be easily distinguished by the broad, brown bands on the exterior.

It is an attractive plant which should be more widely grown in rock gardens and similar situations. It flourishes in lime-free garden soil in full sun provided it can be given adequate moisture. Propagation is by seed and rosette cuttings.

Gentiana nipponica Maxim.

A smallish Japanese species which grows in moist, grassy places at altitudes of around 2,500m (8,200 ft). It is a branching plant, loose in

Plate 9

This plate brings together several well-known and less well-known species, some of them of garden value.

Above left: *Gentiana froelichii*, the Karawanken gentian, is not easy in cultivation. It resents root disturbance, and should be planted out when young.

Above right: *G. algida*, the Arctic gentian, grows in the Arctic regions. This photograph was taken in the Canadian Yukon.

Centre left and centre right: *G. asclepiadea* 'Alba' and *G. asclepiadea* are good garden plants which should be grown more often. Their late flowering is a special asset. Young plants can be established without difficulty in light shade or even in sunless places. There is also a pretty pink form.

Below left: The marsh gentian, *G. pneumonanthe*, is a highly variable plant. In the garden all its types require acid soil and are not easy to cultivate.

Below right: *G. tibetica* from the Himalayas is an easy garden plant, though of a somewhat coarse and unattractive appearance.

habit, with numerous straggling non-flowering shoots and two or three more or less erect flowering shoots each carrying one to three stalkless flowers or occasionally more. The largest leaves—those at the base of the flowering shoots—are only 0.6cm (¼ in) long; they are thick in texture with recurved margins, in shape ovate with blunt points. The leaves of the barren shoots are even smaller and narrower. The flowers are tubular, purplish-blue, and up to 2cm (¾ in) long. The overall height of the plant is 5 to 10cm (2 to 4 in). It flowers in August and is propagated by seed.

Though not a striking plant it is one which the enthusiast will wish to grow. It should be given a moist place in the rock garden; in exposed districts winter protection is advisable. Closely related to *G. jamesii*, it sometimes occurs in association with it in the wild. There is another type known as *G. nipponica* 'Yezoense'.

Gentiana nubigena see *G. algida*

Gentiana ochroleuca see *G. villosa*

Plate 10

The display of gentians begins in late spring with the low-growing species from the European Alps, and continues until the first frost brings an end to the flowering of the Chinese species.

Above: *Gentiana septemfida* is perhaps the most important summer-flowering gentian.

Centre left: The picture shows a small part of a clump of *G. septemfida*. This name comprises various different forms.

Centre right: *G. gelida* is closely related to *G. septemfida*. Its flowers are whitish-yellow and in the garden, like *G. septemfida*, it requires a sunny place and fairly heavy soil.

Below left: A comparatively novel garden plant is *G. paradoxa* from the Caucasus, valuable for its late flowers which do not appear until September.

Below right: Another species from the Caucasus is *G. pyrenaica*, sometimes known as *G. djimilensis*. This photograph was taken on Mount Elbrus at 2,800m (9,200 ft). An extremely difficult plant in cultivation. The type from the Pyrenees, after which the species is named, is somewhat smaller.

Gentiana occidentalis Jakowatz (western gentian)

A member of the *acaulis* group found in the western Pyrenees and Cantabrian mountains, where it occurs on limestone subsoils. The leaves are elliptical to oblong-lanceolate. The calyx teeth are usually more than half as long as the tube, ovate to lanceolate, narrowed at the base. Its splendid, deep-blue flowers, which appear in June, have few or no green spots in the throat; the corolla lobes are acute to acuminate. Morphologically, it is roughly intermediate between *G. clusii* and *G. angustifolia*. Seldom seen in gardens, though not difficult to grow.

Gentiana olivieri Griseb.

A native of Asia Minor, also widely distributed in Kurdistan, Syria, Iraq, Iran and even in the Himalayas. It forms a rosette made up of numerous leaves up to 12cm (5 in) long and only 1.3cm (½ in) wide, spoon shaped and tapering at the base into a stalk. The stem leaves are few in number, and the topmost pair clasp the lower parts of the flower. The rosettes put up one to three flowering stems, about 23cm (9 in) long, spreading at the base but later upright. At their tops is a cluster of three to nine flowers in a cyme or umbel. The topmost flowers are unstalked, but those at the sides have stalks. The flowers are bell shaped and deep blue, the corolla being twice as long as the calyx. The flowering season is at the end of June or beginning of July. It is propagated by seed.

This species is probably not hardy everywhere and will require winter protection. A well-drained spot in full sun is necessary.

Gentiana oregana Engelm. ex A. Gray

An American species found in western and northern California, Oregon and British Columbia. A robust plant with flowering stems over 30cm (12 in) tall carrying several bell-shaped, purplish-blue flowers widely open at their mouths. The leaves are broadly ovate or oblong, about 3cm (1⅛ in) long, arranged in pairs clasping the stem. Closely related to *G. affinis*, this species can be distinguished by its oblong or ovate calyx lobes, equal in length to the calyx tube, and by its broad, bell-shaped corolla. In *G. affinis* the calyx lobes are unequal, and only the longest lobe is as long as the tube; the flowers are narrow tubular. The flowering time is August.

This species is not difficult in cultivation, and is an interesting plant which the enthusiast will wish to have in his collection. It demands lime-free soil with added peat or leafmould and adequate moisture.

Gentiana oreodoxa H. Smith

A perennial species from China which has recently been re-introduced into cultivation. It grows to a height of 5 to 12cm (2 to 4¾ in) and has blue flowers 3 to 4cm (1³⁄₁₆ to 1⅝ in) in diameter.

Gentiana ornata Wallich ex Griseb.

A native of Nepal, where it was discovered in the nineteenth century. It forms a basal rosette with leaves about 2.5cm (1 in) long, spreading from which are numerous slender, brownish semi-prostrate shoots. These are much shorter than those of its Chinese counterpart *G. sino ornata*, being only 10cm (4 in) long. They carry pairs of narrow leaves up to 12mm (½ in) long. The solitary, erect flowers are at the ends of the shoots. The calyx is about 2.5cm (1 in) long, roughly two-thirds of its length being made up by the tube. The calyx lobes are linear and considerably shorter than the tube. The broad, bell-shaped corolla is blue with a pale-whitish interior. On the outside there are five broad purplish-blue stripes with creamy-white between them. Flowering begins at the end of August and continues into September, the flowers remaining open even on wet, cloudy days. It is indeed a treasure in the garden and is not difficult to grow. All it requires is good lime-free garden soil in an open sunny position. It is best propagated by division, though this is not as productive as in certain similar species; it can also be raised from seed with inevitable variation displayed in the offspring.

Another plant recently offered is *G. ornata* var. *congestifolia*. Also a native of Nepal, this grows to a height of 6 to 8cm (up to 3¼ in) and flowers in July to September. It has enamel-blue flowers, white inside with speckled throats, externally with purple-blue stripes and creamy-white areas between them. The flowers remain open in bad weather. The corolla is more club shaped than in the type species. However, the plants offered are not always genuine.

Gentiana oschtenica Kusn. see *G. verna* var. *oschtenica*

Gentiana pannonica Scop. (Hungarian gentian, brown gentian)

Found in the eastern Alps from north-eastern Switzerland to north-western Yugoslavia, Bavarian Forest, Bohemian Forest, Carpathians and Transylvania. Grows on meadows and pastures, screes and the grassy bottoms of alpine corries, among dwarf pine and in forests, even around cowherds' huts. It occurs both on limestone and acid rock. It has a stout, oblique, multiheaded rootstock with many elliptical basal leaves narrowing towards their stalks and several stems 15 to 60cm (6 to 24 in) tall, sometimes tinged with purple, carrying several pairs of stem leaves. The latter are ovate to lanceolate, 7.5cm (3 in) long or more, and clasp the stem. The flowers are situated in the upper leaf axils and are grouped into clusters or pseudo-whorls at the top. The bell-shaped calyx is only one-fourth the length of the corolla and has five to eight lobes bent outwards. The bell-shaped, widely open corolla has five to nine obovate lobes roughly 1.5cm (½ in) long, its total length being 2.5 to 5.5cm (1 to 2¼ in). In colour it is a mixture of dull or bluish-purple merging into yellowish-green near the base with reddish-black spots; internally the flowers are yellowish and unspotted. The overall impression is of a purplish-brown colour. Flowering time is July to August.

G. pannonica is closely related to *G. punctata* and *G. purpurea*, though easily distinguished from them by its flower colour. When out of flower it can be distinguished from *G. punctata* by the curve of the calyx lobes on the flower buds.

Its garden value is a matter of opinion. The plant is not exactly beautiful and its dusky flower colour is not comparable with the true gentian blue, yet it is not without a certain charm. Cultivation presents little difficulty, deep soil in full sun being sufficient, and although the species sometimes occurs on limestone, in the garden it seems to prefer neutral to slightly acid soil. It can be propagated by seed (very slow) or division of older plants.

Gentiana paradoxa Alboff (sometimes spelt Albov)

A native, and indeed an endemic, of the mountains of the western Caucasus extending to the Colchis. Generally on basic soil. A perennial 30 to 40cm (12 to 16 in) tall with straight stems and narrow linear leaves. The flowers are comparatively large 4 to 5cm long (1½ to 2 in), pale to middle-blue, and almost white inside the corolla. The corolla has asymmetrical folds in the secondary corolla lobes. The flowering season is relatively long, extending from the end of August to mid-October.

A recent arrival in cultivation, it is an excellent garden plant and must be welcomed. The blue coloration seems to vary under differing light conditions. It is propagated by seed.

Gentiana parryi Engelm.

Grows in the alpine and subalpine zones of the mountains of Colorado, New Mexico, Utah and Wyoming. Some botanists do not accept it as a true species and assign it to *G. affinis*. It forms upright clumps of stems

30 to 45cm (12 to 18 in) tall. The stem leaves are arranged in pairs, and are 3.5 to 4cm (1⅜ to 1⅝ in) long, broad ovate, thick in texture with rough margins and clasping the stem. At the tops of the stems are one to five unstalked flowers, the topmost pair of leaves forming a cup at the base of the flower cluster. The calyx tube is entire or has only a slight split on one side. The calyx lobes are linear and considerably shorter than the tube. The corolla is bell shaped, about 4cm (1⅝ in) long, with upright broad ovate or obovate lobes which are abruptly pointed. The flower colour is purplish-blue. The species is easily recognised by its linear calyx lobes; those of the closely related *G. calycosa* are ovate.

It is a good garden plant, easily grown in lime-free soil of adequate moisture-holding capacity in a sunny spot, and is propagated by seed. Flowering time is from August to the beginning of September. Unfortunately, the plants offered in the trade and the seeds in the seed exchanges are not always genuine.

Gentiana platypetala Griseb.

A species from the coastal regions of Alaska southwards to British Columbia, where it grows in alpine turf above the treeline in open situations. Arising from the rhizome-like roots are stems 20 to 40cm (8 to 16 in) tall which are clasped by paired leaves, ovate to elliptic in shape, about 3.5cm (1½ in) long. The plant is distinguished by the divided, bract-like calyx; one part has two teeth and the other has three. The tubular, blue flowers with green spots in their interior appear in July to August. Though not often offered, this species is well worth a trial. It grows in ordinary garden soils and can be propagated by seed or cautious division.

Gentiana pneumonanthe L. (marsh gentian)

A gentian with an enormous range extending throughout almost the whole of Europe into Western Asia and southwards to the Caucasus. Because of its wide distribution it is highly variable. For example, though most plants are between 20 and 40cm (8 and 16 in) tall, some are as low as 10cm (4 in) and others as high as 60cm (24 in). The plant does not form a basal leaf rosette, but has cataphylls or scale leaves, from the axils of which spring the upright leafy stems which are blunt angled and usually unbranched. There are variations in leaf shape and flower colour as well as in height. The leaves are for the most part linear or linear-lanceolate, 25 to 53mm (1 to 2 in) long, narrowed at the base and slightly recurved, arranged in pairs. The flowers are of impressive appearance, 4 to 5cm (1½ to 2 in) long, carried in twos or threes at the ends of the stems and singly in the leaf axils, numbering up to ten on each stem, the lower flowers having distinct stalks. The calyx is bell shaped with five linear, sharply pointed teeth. The corolla is erect, bell shaped or funnel shaped, deep purplish-blue, rarely pale blue with five green-spotted stripes on the exterior. There are also pink and white forms. The flowering season is July to August.

Various types have been described (*G. pneumonanthe* var. *minor*, var. *latifolia*, var. *depressa*, var. *diffusa*), though not all are recognised by botanists.

In the wild it grows in boggy meadows, fens, moist heaths and sandy or peaty clearings in woods, invariably on acid soil. Rarely cultivated in gardens, it is not an easy plant; it requires a moist place and lime-free soil enriched with peat or leaf mould. In cultivation it is not long lived. It can be propagated by seed and will usually flower in its second year.

Gentiana pontica see *G. verna* ssp. *pontica*

Gentiana prolata Balf. f.

A native of the Himalaya, in particular Sikkim, Bhutan and south-east Tibet. In the past often confused with *G. ornata*, although clearly distinct from the latter. It forms loose mats consisting of numerous shoots about 15cm (6 in) long. Except when very young, it does not form leaf rosettes. The slender shoots carry numerous narrow leaflets about 12mm (½ in) long arranged in pairs. The calyx is 13 to 14mm (about ½ in) long. The corolla is 3.2cm (1¼ in) long and about 4cm (1⅝ in) wide. The flowers are blue with broad, purplish stripes on the exterior and creamy-white zones between them. The corolla lobes are not spreading as in *G. farreri* and other species, but erect. This species is distinguished from its relatives by the smallness of its overall dimensions and its flowers, and also by the shape of the flowers. Flowering time is August to October.

A plant for the enthusiast, it is not too difficult in cultivation. It should be grown in ordinary lime-free garden soil in full sun and provided with adequate moisture during the growing period. It is propagated by seed and cuttings, but the plants offered by nurseries are not always true.

Gentiana przewalskii Maxim.

A native of north-western China and north-eastern Tibet where it grows on alpine pastures, reaching a height of up to 25cm (10 in). It is similar in certain respects to *G. algida* and *G. frigida*, with which it has sometimes been confused. It forms lax rosettes and barren shoots with several pairs of leaves. The lower leaves are narrow spatulate and up to 7.5cm (3 in) long; the stem leaves are smaller, and the fertile shoots carry several terminal flowers. The calyx is cylindrical, roughly 1.8cm (¾ in) long; the corolla is white tinged and streaked with blue, and 5cm (2 in) long. Flowering time is from July to October.

Often regarded as a variety of *G. algida*, it is interesting rather than beautiful. In cultivation it is not easy; it requires perfect drainage and stony soil or scree. It is propagated by seed or by dividing older plants.

Gentiana puberulenta Pringle

SYNONYMS: *G. puberula* non Michx., *Dasystephana puberula* (Michx.) Small.

This gentian is found in prairies and other grassy places from Manitoba and Ontario and southwards to Kansas and Arkansas. It is relatively uncommon. The stems, 20 to 50cm (8 to 20 in) tall, are often covered with fine hairs. The leaves are oblong lanceolate, sometimes linear, coarsely or finely hairy along their margins and the central vein. The flowers, whitish below and blue above, are 3 to 4cm (1⅛ to 1½ in) long and one to six in number and are carried in clusters at the top of the stem and the upper leaf axils. They are described as vase shaped. Flowering time is July to October. There are also violet and white types. A pretty plant, but not long lived. Propagated by seed, it likes full sun and a fairly dry place with good drainage. The similar species *G. affinis* has upright corolla lobes and unequal calyx lobes.

Gentiana pumila Jacq. (dwarf gentian)

SYNONYM: *G. verna* L. var. *pumila* Arcangeli

A native of the south-eastern limestone Alps including the Venetian Alps where it occurs here and there on short turf and in stony places, in moist spots and snowpatch depressions, invariably on limestone. In nature it is accompanied by *Primula clusiana*, *Dryas octopetala*, *Globularia cordifolia*, *Androsace villosa*, *Armeria alpina* and *Saxifraga aizoides*. The plant forms small tufts 3 to 8cm (1¼ to 3¼ in) tall consisting of flowering and non-flowering shoots 5cm (2 in) long, the flowers being invariably solitary. The leaves of the basal rosette are linear-lanceolate, tapering to a point, often narrowing towards the base. The stems are short and carry one to three leaf pairs. The calyx is tubular bell shaped, 8 to 15mm (⅜ to ⅝ in) long, with narrow wings, sometimes tinged with violet. The calyx teeth are linear-lanceolate, almost as long as the tube. The saucer-shaped corolla is sky blue. In the wild it flowers from June to August.

Flora Europaea distinguishes two subspecies. *G. pumila* ssp. *pumila* has a calyx 11 to 14mm (7⁄16 to 9⁄16 in) long with acute calyx lobes (eastern Alps), while *G. pumila* ssp. *delphinensis* (Beauverd) P. Fourn. (syn. *G. delphinensis* Beauverd) has a calyx 16 to 20mm (5⁄8 to 13⁄16 in) long with lobes which are obtuse, sometimes apiculate (south-western Alps and eastern Pyrenees).

A pretty species, but not easy in cultivation. It demands full sun and soil containing plenty of limestone rubble. Similar conditions are necessary in the alpine house. Some of the older writers suggest a compost of peat, sand and coal dust. A plant for connoisseurs and enthusiasts.

Gentiana punctata L. (spotted gentian)

Found in the Alps, the Sudeten mountains, the Carpathians and in the Balkans southwards to southern Bulgaria. In the western Alps it extends as far as Salzburg and Carinthia, and in Germany it is found in the Allgäu and Berchtesgaden Alps. Widely distributed on stony pastures and grazing, the grassy bottoms of mountain corries, screes and moraines, among rhododendrons and in conifer woods, usually between 1,500 and 2,500m (4,900 and 8,200 ft). Occurring both on limestone and igneous rocks, it prefers deep loamy soils. It has a thick rootstock with roots up to 1m (1 yd) long. It is a sturdy, upright plant, 20 to 60cm (8 to 24 in) tall, with several unbranched stems bearing glossy, ovate-elliptic, pointed, five-veined, opposite leaves, the lower leaves being stalked and the upper sessile. The flowers are carried in clusters in the upper leaf axils and at the tops of the stems. The erect corolla is bell shaped, open at the mouth, with five to eight short, blunt lobes, pale yellow in colour with dark spots. The bell-shaped calyx is one-third the length of the corolla. Flowering time is from July to September.

Given deep soil and full sun, it is easily managed in the garden. Propagated by seed, the young plants should be put out with root-balls when very young. An interesting plant, though of no great beauty, suitable for the larger rock garden.

Gentiana purpurea L. (purple gentian)

Found in the Alps from Savoy through Switzerland and Northern Italy, and north-eastwards as far as Vorarlberg and the Allgäu, also in the Apennines and southern Norway, usually from 1,600 to 2,700m (5,260 to 8,800 ft), though occasionally at lower altitudes. Scattered, usually in small groups, on meadows, pastures and the grassy bottoms of mountain corries, sometimes in scrub and thin, conifer woodland. In nature it is accompanied by *Athyrium distentifolium*, *Astrantia minor*, *Arnica montana*, *Aconitum paniculatum*, *Saxifraga rotundifolia* and *Campanula rhomboidalis*, usually on lime-free soils.

An erect perennial 20 to 60cm (8 to 24 in) tall, with hollow stems bearing ovate-lanceolate, five-veined, opposite leaves, the lower leaves being stalked and the upper sessile. The large, erect sessile flowers are carried in clusters of five to ten at the top of the stem, though sometimes they develop in the upper leaf axils only. The flowers are bell shaped, somewhat expanded towards the top, with five to eight blunt corolla lobes. Externally they are purplish-red and internally yellowish with purple spots. Flowering time is July to September. Easily distinguished from related species by the large, split, sheath-like calyx and the blunt corolla lobes which are broadest at the middle.

Though it cannot compete in beauty and garden merit with the blue-flowered species, *G. purpurea* is more attractive than some of its relatives. In culture it seldom exceeds 45cm (18 in) in height, and is easily grown in sandy, lime-free soil enriched with peat. *G. purpurea* 'Nana', roughly 25cm (10 in) tall, is commercially available.

Gentiana pyrenaica L. (Pyrenian gentian)

SYNONYMS: *G. dschimilensis* C. Koch, often spelt *G. dijlgensis* or *G. dshimilensis*.

This gentian has remarkably disfunct distribution, being found in the Pyrenees, the Carpathians, in Bulgaria and Macedonia, in the Caucasus, in Turkish Armenia and in Iran. A pretty little plant which forms tufts a little over 7cm (2¾ in) tall with glossy, linear green leaves 2.5cm (1 in) long. The single, stiffly erect, terminal flowers are violet-blue inside and usually greenish outside. The funnel-shaped flowers are somewhat similar to those of the *acaulis* group and reach dimensions of 3.4 to 4 cm (1¼ to 1½ in). The plicae are equal in size to the corolla lobes. Flowering time is June to July.

Usually found on mountain slopes, in the Pyrenees it occurs at lower altitudes (usually below 1,500m (4,900 ft)) in wet, peaty or heathy spots, in the Caucasus in drier places in humus-filled depressions at altitudes of 2,800m (9,200 ft) or more.

This is one of the most difficult species in cultivation and so far only a few experts have successfully established it. It is propagated by seed. Because of its meagre growth in cultivation, division is scarcely feasible. Having seen *G. pyrenaica* in full flower on Mount Elbrus in the Caucasus at 3,000m (9,800 ft), the writer feels that it would justify every effort to bring it into cultivation in lowland gardens.

The Caucasian form is known as G. *djimilensis* C. Koch, but does not really deserve specific rank, the only difference being that the whole plant is somewhat more robust.

Gentiana rostanii Reuter ex Verlot

Pyrenees, Western Alps, Piedmont, growing in wet meadows. Closely related to *G. bavarica*; it could be described as a narrow-leaved form, the lower leaves being rather crowded and the upper leaves more distant. All the leaves are four times as long as wide. The calyx is toothed and the flowers blue. Seldom seen in cultivation, it requires stony soil with adequate moisture in full sun. Not easy. Flowering time June to September.

Gentiana rubicaulis Schweinitz

A native of North America, found chiefly in the region of the Great Lakes and Hudson's Bay. It is one of the 'closed' gentians, very similar to *G. linearis*. It has reddish or purplish stems 30 to 70cm (12 in to 2 ft 4 in) tall with fleshy, ovate, pale-green leaves up to 7.5cm (3 in) long. The species is readily recognised by the long, upper internodes. The flowers are carried in clusters of up to 15 at the tops of the stems or in the upper leaf axils. The tubular corolla is pale violet to white, 3.5 to 4cm (1¼ to 1½ in) long. There are also types with ivory-coloured, blue and pink-tinged flowers. It flowers in July to September. In the garden it will probably prefer half shade and adequate dampness. As it occurs on limestone and acid soils, soil reaction is not critical in cultivation. Propagation is by seed.

Gentiana saponaria L.

SYNONYM: *G. puberula* Michx.

This species is found in damp woods from Pennsylvania to Illinois and northwards as far as Alaska and Labrador. In the garden it grows up to 90cm (3 ft) tall with one or a few stems. The leaves are linear-lanceolate to broad elliptic. The flowers (up to 8) are carried in terminal and axillary racemes. The calyx is tubular, with linear oblanceolate lobes up to 12mm (½ in) long, equal in length to the tube. The corolla is club-shaped, 3.5 to 4cm (1¼ to 1½ in) long, blue with green spots inside. It flowers from August to mid-November. The flowers remain almost closed; only in the eastern part of its range do they open slightly more widely.

In cultivation it requires a moist place in half shade on lime-free soil. Propagation is by seed. In the garden, contrary to its behaviour in nature, it is shy flowering.

Gentiana saxosa G. Forst.

A New Zealand species, found in South Island and Stewart Island, where it grows on sandhills near the coast. From a deep root it puts up numerous, branched, prostrate stems turning upright at their tips. At flowering time the plant is only 5 to 7cm (2 to 3 in) in overall height. The basal leaves are spatulate, up to 3.6cm (1½ in) long and brownish-green or dark green. The stem leaves are similar in shape but smaller and with shorter stalks. All the leaves, both basal and stem leaves, are fleshy. The stems measure some 15cm (6 in) in overall length. The stalked flowers are carried in terminal clusters of two to five. The calyx is one-third of the length of the corolla and is split for one-third of its length. The corolla is white with greenish veins, broadly bell shaped, and 12mm (½ in) long. Flowering time is in August.

G. saxosa is a pretty plant and deserves to be more widely grown, even though it is not very long lived. Of all New Zealand gentians this is the species most often seen in cultivation. It likes full sun and stony lime-free soil with good drainage but adequate moisture. It is easily raised from seed.

Gentiana scabra Bunge

Northern Asia and Japan. This species is variable in its appearance and has sometimes been the source of some confusion, especially among plants from Japan. It has more or less erect leafy stems about 30cm (12 in) long. The leaves are ovate with rough margins and central veins. The base of each leaf pair clasps the stem. The internodes are of the same length as the leaves. The flowers are carried in racemes of four to five in the upper leaf axils and the ends of the stems, and are always unstalked. The calyx is tubular, 10 to 12mm (about ½ in) long; the lobes are unequal, linear-oblong and about the same length as the tube. The bell-shaped corolla is over 2.5cm (1 in) long; the corolla lobes are broad ovate, sharply pointed and five times as long as the plicae. The flowers are deep blue, some varieties showing pronounced spotting in the tube and on the corolla lobes. Flowering time is late, often not starting until September. There are numerous varieties of which the following may be mentioned: *G. scabra* var. *buergeri* (Miq.) Maxim (sometimes spelt *G. scabra* var. *burgeri*) grows up to 90cm (3 ft) or taller and has 10 to 20 pairs of stem leaves. The flowers are up to 6cm (2⅜ in) long, mid-blue in colour and somewhat reminiscent of those of *G. asclepiadea*. *Flora of Japan* by Ohwi lists the following synonyms: *G. buergeri* Miq., *G. scabra* var. *intermedia* Kusn., *G. scabra* var. *buergeri* subvar. *saxatilis* Honda, *G. saxatilis* (Honda) Honda, *G. scabra* var. *orientalis* Hara, *G. subpetiolata* Honda. Another variety more often seen in cultivation is *G. scabra* var. *fortunei*, with conspicuous spotting in the interior of the flowers. *G. scabra* var. *procumbens* has prostrate stems which will even hang down when the plant is grown in a suitable place. Lesser known varieties include *G. scabra* var. *bungeana*, *G. scabra* var. *buergeri* f. *stenophylla*. Japanese nurseries offer a pink form known as *G. scabra* 'Rosea'.

In 1963 the Japanese botanist Toyakuni made a special study of these variations and proposed the following classification:

G. scabra Bunge var. *buergeri* (Rindo-gentian), *G. scabra* Bunge subvar. *buergeri* Maxim. (Tsukushi rindo), *G. scabra* Bunge f. *saxatilis* Toyokuni (Kumagawa rindo), *G. scabra* Bunge f. *procumbens* Toyokuni (Kirishima rindo), *G. scabra* subvar. *orientalis* Toyokuni (Sasa rindo, Tonashi rindo) (of considerable commercial importance in Japan as a pot plant) and *G. scabra* f. *stenophylla* Toyokuni (Hosoba rindo).

It is propagated by seed. Unfortunately, many other species masquerade under the name *G. scabra*. For purposes of identification it should be noted that *G. scabra* does not have basal leaf rosettes (in contrast to *G. crassicaule* and *G. cruciata*, which are often distributed under its name). It is a robust species of considerable garden value, especially in the form *G. scabra* var. *buergeri*.

Gentiana sceptrum Griseb.

SYNONYMS: *G. menziesii* A. Gray, *G. orfordii* T. J. Howell

A native of the western side of North America, from California to British Columbia, where it grows in moist places, sphagnum bogs and swamps in woods. Arising from a robust root stock its stems are 40 to 60cm (16 to 24 in) and sometimes over 1m (3 ft) in height, though in the garden considerably less. The paired stem leaves are lanceolate to linear-lanceolate, 3.5 to 6.5cm (1½ to 2½ in) long and somewhat more than half that in breadth. The flowers are both terminal and axillary and are carried on short side stems. They are grouped in twos or threes on very short stalks which are clasped by the uppermost pair of leaves. The calyx is 1.2 to 1.8cm (½ to ¾ in) long. The corolla is tubular-bell shaped, dark blue, often with greenish spots. The corolla lobes are erect and broadly ovate with rounded tips. The flowering time is August.

This species is one of the finest American gentians and is not difficult in cultivation provided it has moist lime-free soil. The seed offered is not always true, and often turns out to be from *G. septemfida*.

Gentiana septemfida Pall.

SYNONYM: *G. cordifolia* C. Koch

This species has a wide range throughout Asia Minor, Iran, the Eastern Caucasus, the Altai and Turkestan. As might be expected, it varies widely in form and appearance, and these variations sometimes cause confusion. In the wild it grows at subalpine and alpine altitudes, in various habitats, mostly dry.

The plants consist of several upright or spreading leafy stems, usually 20 to 30cm (8 to 12 in) long. The ovate stem leaves are placed in pairs at short intervals; they are distinctly five or seven-veined, the uppermost leaves being about 3.2cm (1¼ in) long and 1.2cm (½ in) wide, usually pointed. The flowers are carried in close terminal clusters of up to eight blossoms. The calyx is tubular, 1.2cm (½ in) long, with five equal linear lobes roughly as long as the tube. The corolla is bell shaped, five lobed, the plicae being deeply cut into many divisions. The flowers are blue with a whitish throat marked with darker stripes and spots. The flowering time is from July to August.

From the botanical name, the flowers might be expected to be divided into seven parts, but this is by no means the rule, although an odd flower with seven lobes can sometimes be found. The true species is not widely found in gardens, most of the plants bearing this name belonging to one of the following varieties or forms.

G. septemfida f. *olivana* was raised by one of the early enthusiasts of alpine gardening, Erich Wocke, at Oliva near Danzig. It is a plant of tight, erect habit, 12–15cm (5–6 in) tall, with heads of many dark-blue blossoms, most of which have six or seven lobes.

G. septemfida var. *cordifolia* (Koch) Boiss. may not be a valid name and may merely be a garden form with prostrate stems, bluntly cordate leaves and less numerous, smaller flowers, speckled with white on the inside.

However, there is no doubt as to the botanical standing of *G. septemfida* var. *lagodechiana* Kusn. (syn. *G. lagodechiana* hort.) which grows in moist, rocky places in the eastern Caucasus. It has prostrate stems 30cm (12 in) long turning upwards at their tips. Unlike *G. septemfida*, this variety has solitary flowers—terminal and axillary. It has a long flowering season from July to September.

Another widely distributed form is *G. septemfida* 'Doeringiana', a compact plant of upright growth with relatively large, deep-blue flowers. Unfortunately, this form has often been propagated by seed, with the result that a ragbag of different types is in circulation under this name. The genuine type tends to spread sideways and requires ample space—about 50cm (20 in) between plants. Useful for cut flowers.

Gentiana 'Hascombensis' is widely grown in Great Britain. It is a selected form derived from a cross between *G. septemfida* f. *latifolia* and *G. septemfida* var. *lagodechiana*. It has upright stems about 30cm (12 in) tall carrying many-flowered clusters of narrow, bell-shaped flowers somewhat lighter in colour than the type, with speckling in the interior.

G. freyniana sometimes goes under the name *G. septemfida* var. *freyniana*, but it should be accepted as a species in its own right.

G. septemfida and its related forms are some of the most easily cultivated gentian species, and well-established plants can look really splendid. It prefers ordinary garden soil and requires full sun; in a shady position it becomes less attractive. Propagation is by division, cuttings and seed; but plants raised from seed tend to vary, unless the seed has been obtained from the wild. It is a good plant for the rock garden and for low edgings. Among the numerous garden plants which can be associated with it are *Geum* hybrids, *Geranium dalmaticum*, *Leontopodium alpinum*, *Dryas*, *Saponaria ocymoides*, *Silene schafta* 'Splendens' and *Sedum album* 'Coral Carpet'.

Gentiana setigera A. Gray

Found in moist places in the coastal regions of Northern California. It has several stems up to 30cm (12 in) tall, prostrate at the base then turning upright, with ovate to rounded leaves up to 6cm (2⅜ in) long. The shorter stems carry a single terminal flower, but the stouter, longer stems have up to five, each of them having a pair of leaves at the base. The flowers are blue or purplish blue, broad tubular, and roughly 3.6 to 4cm (1 7/16 to 1 9/16 in) long. *G. setigera* can be distinguished from other species by its spreading stems, the open corolla and the threadlike structure of the plicae.

It requires lime-free peaty soil with adequate moisture. It is propagated by seed or division of older plants. Doubtfully hardy in Europe.

Gentiana sikkimensis C. B. Clarke

A native of western China, south-eastern Tibet and Sikkim, where it grows mainly on moist, stony slopes. It forms mats of numerous shoots up to 15cm (6 in) long or more. The glossy stem leaves are in pairs, oblong or wedge-shaped, and up to 2.5cm (1 in) long. The flowers are arranged in terminal clusters surrounded by the uppermost leaves. The calyx is tubular, up to 7mm (¼ in) long, split at one side and has five unequal lobes. The corolla is tubular funnel-shaped, 1.8 to 2cm (about ¾ in) long, blue with a white throat. An attractive garden plant, it flowers profusely from July to August. In cultivation it is not difficult and will grow in any ordinary garden soil provided it has adequate moisture. Propagation is by seed and division. A white-flowered form is also in cultivation (*G. sikkimensis* 'Alba').

Gentiana sikokiana Maxim.

A Japanese species similar in appearance to a slender *G. pneumonanthe*, found in only a few locations on the islands of Sikoki and Kyushu and in the Kinki province of Honshu, mainly in mountain forests. It has slender upright stems 7 to 20cm (2¾ to 8 in) tall with paired, oval-elliptic or spathulate leaves, the lower leaves being stalked and the upper leaves unstalked. They are up to 7.5cm (3 in) long, slightly undulate, three veined and pale green below. The flowers are carried at the tops of the stems, usually in threes, and in ones or twos in the axils of the upper leaves. The terminal flowers are surrounded by the leaves, but the axillary flowers are usually stalked. The corolla is tubular, over 3.7cm (1½ in) in length, with broadly ovate lobes. In colour it is blue or purplish-blue and spotted. The species can be distinguished from the closely related *G. scabra* by its broadly ovate calyx lobes.

Propagation in by seed or by cuttings from the young shoots. It grows satisfactorily in well-drained spots in half shade, but in colder regions with severe frosts it will require protection.

Gentiana sino ornata Balf. f. (Chinese autumn-flowering gentian)

Found in moist places in the mountains of Tibet and western Yunnan, notably the Lichiang range. When it flowered for the first time in the Edinburgh Botanic Garden in 1912—from seeds sent home by Forrest —it aroused great interest. Though related to *G. ornata*, it flowers later, is of a darker blue and grows more vigorously when given a place which suits it. *G. sino ornata* is easily distinguished from *G. ornata* by its tubular corolla more than 6.5cm (2½ in) in length; the corolla of *G. ornata* is short and bell shaped, being only 3.5 to 4cm (1⅜ to 1 9/16 in) long.

It forms a central rosette radiating from which are many prostrate shoots which root at their nodes. The leaves on these shoots or stolons are linear, tapering to a fine point, dark green and rather stiff. The solitary terminal flowers are funnel shaped, deep azure-blue inside, though on the outside their colour is duller and there are broad, purplish stripes. The calyx is less than 3.5cm (1⅜ in) long and the calyx lobes are like the leaves in shape, broad at the base and tapering to a fine tip. An extremely attractive plant for the garden, it grows vigorously in slightly moist soil provided it is entirely free from lime. This species detests lime perhaps more ardently than any other gentian; it cannot stand even the slightest trace. Attempts to grow it in soil which is not completely lime-free offer little prospect of success. Another important requirement is full midday sun.

A garden form of special value is *G. sino ornata* 'Praecox' which flowers some three weeks earlier than the type. The brilliant blue flowers of this strain are visible from afar and make a splendid picture for several weeks, starting in September and sometimes continuing as late as November. It is useful for cut flowers, as the stalks are somewhat taller than those of the species.

The plants should be set out relatively close together so as to produce large uniform patches. Plantings 30cm (12 in) apart will produce

Plate 11

The gentians on this plate show the worldwide distribution of the genus.

Above left: New Zealand has a number of species. Not all of them are in cultivation, but there are some which are quite frequently seen. One such species, *Gentiana saxosa*, is illustrated here.

Above right: *G. newberryi* comes from the Sierra Nevada of California, Nevada and Oregon.

Middle left: *G. cachemirica* is a species from the Himalaya. It is a good garden plant and feels at home in a sunny position in the joints of a dry stone wall.

Centre right: *G. bigelovii* from the Rocky Mountains is a comparatively undemanding plant, though perhaps mainly for the enthusiast and collector.

Below left: *G. affinis* is widely distributed throughout North America. It grows in moist places on weakly acid soil and, as might be expected from its wide range, has adapted to provide a variety of forms.

Below right: *G. andrewsii*, also from North America, is one of the species which have 'closed' flowers.

complete cover in one to two years. The flowers will withstand the first night frosts unharmed.

Propagation is generally by vegetative means, though various methods are employed. Most gardeners claim that March or April is the best time for division. It can also be propagated by seed, or by cuttings in early summer.

There are several selected forms of *G. sino ornata*. Apart from 'Praecox', the white *G. sino ornata* 'Alba', though less vigorous, is also widely grown; it requires dividing frequently and should be given a top dressing of rich, peaty soil once or twice a year so as to induce abundant flowering. Another form offered in the trade is *G. sino ornata* 'Behnken', with broad, glossy-green leaves and brilliant cobalt-blue flowers in September–November, growing to about 10cm (4 in). *G. sino ornata* 'Trug's Form' resembles the type species but has flowers of brilliant, deep ultramarine-blue. 'Purdom's Variety' is a particularly vigorous type. 'Angel's Wings', a form offered in Great Britain, has large blue flowers with white stripes. The selected mutation 'Blauer Stern' ('Blue Star') was raised at the Behnken Gentian Nursery, Hamburg; it has

Plate 12

The gentians illustrated here are no longer included in the genus *Gentiana* but have been split off into the related genera *Gentianella* and *Gentianopsis*. Still further reclassifications must be expected in the future. They are certainly not garden plants, and most of them are very short-lived; nevertheless, seed is nowadays sometimes offered in the seed exchanges, and enthusiasts can try to grow them in rock gardens and elsewhere by sowing the seed directly in its final position.

Above: A good sized plant of *Gentianella germanica* is a magnificent sight. The German gentian is not confined to Germany, but occurs throughout central Europe and elsewhere, usually on poor, limey soils.

Below left: *Gentiana campestris*, the field gentian, likes a similar situation, and its range is even wider.

Below right: *Gentianopsis ciliata* (syn. *Gentianella ciliata*), the fringed gentian. This short-lived species is a late flowerer of great charm, but certainly not a garden plant. It is one of the delights which awaits the rambler in the Alps in the autumn.

large, blue, bell-shaped flowers and long stalks. It is sold only as cut flowers, not as plants.

G. sino ornata is of great importance as the parent of numerous hybrids which are listed under the heading 'Gentian Hybrids'.

Among suitable places are the rock garden, raised beds, peat beds, large pans, and even for edgings in wet places. Other garden plants with white flowers make ideal associates (white autumn-flowering crocuses, October saxifrage, early Christmas roses) but it also goes well with *Oxalis magellanica*, *Calceolaria*, *Cardamine trifolia*, *Nierembergia repens*, *Silene schafta* 'Splendens', *Cornus canadensis* and dwarf ferns such as *Cystopteris bulbifera* or *Adiantum venustum*. In the plant trials *G. sino ornata* received the designation of 'a collectors' item'—I can't understand why!

Gentiana siphonantha Maxim. ex Kusn.

A native of Tibet and north-western China, where this gentian grows on rocky slopes and stony open places. It has erect or sloping stems up to 30cm (12 in) tall. The basal leaves are linear-lanceolate, up to 23cm (9 in) long. The stems carry four or five pairs of stem leaves similar in shape to the basal leaves but becoming smaller above. At the tops of the stems and in the upper leaf axils are several flowers in a head or cluster. The calyx is up to 6mm (¼ in) long and has five unequal lobes, usually awl shaped. The corolla is purplish-blue, tubular-funnel shaped and up to 2.5cm (1 in) long, the lobes being ovate-oblong and slightly pointed. It flowers in July–August.

Though seldom seen in cultivation, this species would be worth growing. Propagated by seed, it is not difficult to grow, but requires moist lime-free soil in full sun.

Gentiana stragulata Balf. f. et Forrest

Grows in Yunnan on wet stony pastures. It resembles *G. sikkimensis*, but is larger in all its parts and instead of clustered flower-heads has only one to three flowers on each stem. The tubular flowers are contracted at the throat, deep blue in the interior and purplish-blue outside. The basal leaves are obovate, about 1.5cm (⅝ in) long and have a distinct stalk. The stem leaves, broadly oval with rounded tips, are arranged in pairs. It flowers in July–August. It is not easy in cultivation. The conditions recommended are stony soil, full sun and adequate moisture. It is propagated by seed or basal cuttings.

Gentiana straminea Maxim.

A native of north-eastern Tibet and north-western China, it grows on grassy slopes and alpine meadows up to 3,500m (11,400 ft). It is a robust plant up to 39cm (12 in) tall with distinct basal rosettes consisting of sharply pointed, five-veined, linear-lanceolate leaves 12.5 to 22cm (5 to 9 in) long and about 1.8cm (¾ in) wide. Arising from the rosette are one or two stout flowering stems, about 25cm (10 in) tall. In young plants they spread outwards but later they are upright. Each stem has one, two or three pairs of leaves, about 5cm (2 in) long, clasping the stem at their base. The long-stalked flowers are carried in clusters below the top of the stem. The calyx is about 1.8cm (¾ in) long, split down one side, whitish and papery. The corolla is obconical in shape, greenish-white, pale yellow or straw coloured. It flowers in August to September and is propagated by seed.

Though the plant may appeal to enthusiasts and collectors, and is easy to grow, it is of little garden value.

Gentiana stylophora see *Megacodon stylophora*

Gentiana tergestina see *G. verna* ssp. *tergestina*

Gentiana terglouensis Hacq. (Triglav gentian)

Found in the southern and south-eastern Alps on limestone soils, seldom on igneous rocks, at altitudes of between 1,900 and 2,700m (6,200 and 8,800 ft). Of scattered occurrence on stony patches of grass and pastures. It forms close mats, 3 to 6cm (1⅛ to 2⅜ in) tall, consisting of flowerless or single flowered shoots, 5 to 20cm (2 to 8 in) long, closely covered with overlapping leaves. All the leaves are of almost the same size, 3 to 5mm (⅛ to 3⁄16 in) long, ovate-lanceolate with a cartilaginous tip. The stems are very short, usually less than 1cm (⅜ in) long, with a single terminal flower. The calyx is tubular, 8 to 17mm (5⁄16 to ⅝ in) long, and about half as long as the corolla. The calyx teeth are triangular-lanceolate. The corolla is saucer shaped and deep-azure blue. It flowers in July and August. It can be distinguished from related species by the crowded, overlapping leaves, with rough edges and small membranous points, by its close, tufted habit and by the short-flowering stems. There is also a somewhat more robust type with larger, broad lanceolate leaves, 5 to 8mm (3⁄16 to ½ in) long and 2.5 to 8mm (⅛ to 5⁄16 in) wide (found mainly in the Swiss Alps, which goes under the name *G. terglouensis* ssp. *schleicheri* Vacc. Tutin (synonyms *G. terglouensis* f. *schleicheri* Vacc., *G. schleicheri* Vacc.).

In the garden it should be planted in a limestone scree or a trough. It requires good drainage yet adequate moisture during the growing period. It prefers full sun and an open position. A plant for the enthusiastic grower of high alpines. It is propagated by seed, although cuttings will root but seldom show any vigour.

Gentiana ternifolia Franch.

A native of China, from the Cang Shan range above Dali. This species forms mats of narrow-leaved shoots with upright, pale-blue flowers with darker stripes on the outside. Recently re-introduced into cultivation and offered under two cultivar names *G. ternifolia* 'Cangshan' and *G. ternifolia* 'Dali'.

Gentiana tianshanica Rupr. ex Kusn.

A species with a relatively wide range, being found in Turkestan, Pakistan, Tibet and various places in the Himalaya, where it grows at altitudes of 3,000 to 4,500m (9,800 to 14,700 ft). The basal leaves are linear-lanceolate and up to 7.5cm (3 in) long or more; the stem leaves (two to four pairs) are oblong and 2.5 to 5cm (1 to 2 in) in length. The corolla is purplish-violet and its triangular, outward pointing lobes are blue. The flowers are carried in rounded clusters at the tops of the stems and in the uppermost leaf axils and have long, spreading bracts. Each flower is 2.5cm (1 in) long and tubular-funnel shaped. Flowering time is August.

Though sometimes offered, it is really a plant for the collector. It is propagated by seed.

Gentiana tibetica King ex Hook. f.

From western Nepal, Sikkim, Bhutan and south-eastern Tibet, where it grows on exposed slopes in rather dry situations at 3,700 to 4,500m (12,100 to 14,700 ft). It is a robust, upright plant 20 to 60cm (8 to 24 in) tall. The basal leaves are broad lanceolate, up to 30cm (12 in) long, narrowing below into a winged stalk. The stem leaves are narrower and clasp the stem. The flowers are carried at the top of the stem in a dense raceme partly surrounded by the upper leaves. The corolla is tubular-funnel shaped, 2.5 to 3cm (1 to 1¼ in) in length, with five triangular-oval lobes, each three times as long as the plicae. The calyx is paper-like with a split down one side, and its lobes are finely toothed. Flowering time is August.

A fairly well-known plant with flowers which are usually greyish-white but sometimes greenish or yellowish-white, and nowadays seen in quite a number of gardens. It is propagated by seed and easily grown in ordinary garden soil in a sunny place.

Gentiana trichotoma Kusn.

A species from the borders of China and Tibet. It is a tall perennial 45 to 60cm in height (18 to 24 in) with upright flowering stems, often with a slight purplish-brown tinge. The basal leaves are narrow, about 10cm (4 in) long and 1.2cm (½ in) wide, tapering to the stalk. The stem leaves are much broader in proportion, being some 5cm (2 in) long and 1.2cm (½ in) wide. The flowers, usually in threes, are carried on short stalks in the upper leaf axils and the top of the stem. The corolla is just over 2.5cm (1 in) long, deep blue in colour, whitish inside and spotted with blue. The flower colour is variable and white forms are occasionally seen. It flowers in June and July.

A handsome species but not altogether easy to grow. It requires sandy, lime-free soil, rich in humus, with adequate moisture and half shade. In districts where atmospheric humidity is higher it can be grown in full sun. It is propagated by seed.

Gentiana triflora Pall.

A native of eastern Siberia, Korea, Sakhalin and Japan, where it grows in alpine meadows, this beautiful species has several geographical variants. Botanists subdivide it into *G. triflora* var. *triflora* (eastern Siberia, Korea, Sakhalin), *G. triflora* var. *japonica* (Kusn.), Hara (syn. *G. axillariflora* Lév. et Vaniot), *G. jesoana* Nakai, *G. axillariflora* var. *naitoana* (Lév. et Faurie) Koidx, from Japan and *G. triflora* var. *horomuiensis* (Kudo) Hara, which has linear-lanceolate leaves and occurs in marshy places on the island of Hokkaido.

This species has stems 30 to 80cm (12 in to 2 ft 8 in) tall. The stem leaves are arranged in pairs, each pair at right angles to the next, not forming a tube round the stem. The leaves at the base of the stem are smaller. The flowers are carried in the upper leaf axils and at the top of the stem; the terminal flowers are usually grouped in threes and are unstalked, while those in the leaf axils are single or in twos and have a short stalk. The calyx is undivided or has only one slight slit. The bell-shaped corolla is over 3cm (1³⁄16 in) long, with rounded, ovate, erect lobes. The flowers are dark blue to purplish-blue, and open in August to September. In *G. triflora* var. *japonica* the flowers are solitary or in pairs, and the leaves are thicker and shorter.

In Japan various other forms are recognised: *G. triflora* var. *japonica* f. *crasse*, *G. triflora* var. *japonica* f. *montana* and *G. triflora* var. *japonica* f. *horomuiensis*.

Further varieties are offered commercially: *G. triflora* var. *japonica*, deep blue to purplish-blue, 30 to 80cm (12 in to 2 ft 8 in) tall; *G. triflora* var. *japonica* f. *leucantha* with white flowers; *G. triflora* var. *yezoensis* with bluish-violet flowers (botanically identical with *G. triflora* var. *japonica*).

Propagation is by seed, and it is an excellent plant for open situations on lime-free soil.

In the 1970s a gentian was introduced into the Federal Republic of Germany under the name *Gentiana* 'Royal Blue'. It was the subject of considerable publicity and was promoted especially for commercial nurseries. In response to enquiries regarding its botanical status it was given the name *G. makinoi* 'Royal Blue', and this name appeared in the horticultural journals of that time. However, it is probably an especially fine type of *G. triflora* var. *japonica* (syn. *G. jesoana*). Unfortunately, in many cases growers were not informed that satisfactory cultivation is feasible only in extremely acid soil (pH 3.4 to 3.7); attempts to grow it in weakly acid soil at pH 6.8 led to chlorosis. A compost rich in peat with a good supply of nutrients will ensure good results. Given the necessary growing conditions, it is a valuable plant for commercial growers, as it furnishes a supply of long-stemmed, long-lasting cut flowers with deep-blue blossoms from September to November. Thorough investigations have been carried out by Prof. P. Fischer at the Institute of Soil Science and Plant Nutrition, FH Weihenstephan.

This plant, *G. jesoana* 'Royal Blue', (the correct botanical name is *G. triflora* var. *japonica* 'Royal Blue') has approximately the same requirements as regards pH as does *G. sino ornata*. More recently a white type ('Alba') with pure-white flowers has become available. *G. triflora* var. *japonica* f. *leucantha* has small dark spots in the throat.

Gentiana tubiflora (G. Don) Griseb.

A Himalayan plant, found chiefly in Nepal, Sikkim and western Tibet, where it grows on open hillsides and in scree. A low-growing tufted species, only about 2.5cm (1 in) high, it has barren rosettes set close to the ground and flowering rosettes carrying the upright flowers. The leaflets, crowded along the shoots, are only 0.6cm (¼ in) long, spoon shaped or oblong with sharp points, tapering towards the base. The solitary deep-blue flowers are narrow tubular, up to 2.5cm (1 in) long, with erect triangular or oval lobes. The calyx is somewhat more than half as long as the corolla and has short erect narrow oval lobes.

Not easy in cultivation, it demands stony soil, good drainage and full sun. Propagation is by seed or division.

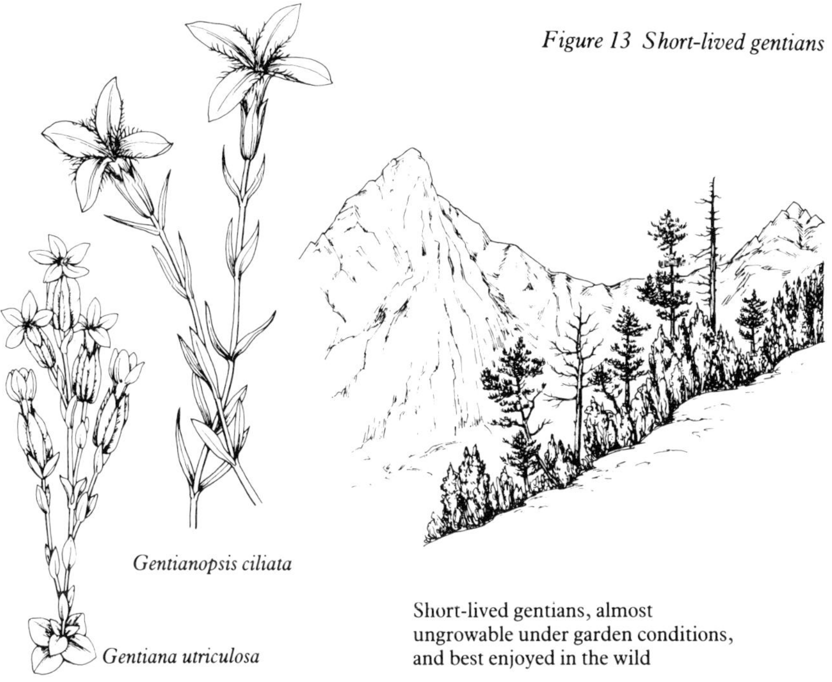

Figure 13 Short-lived gentians

Short-lived gentians, almost ungrowable under garden conditions, and best enjoyed in the wild

Gentiala utriculosa L.

Found in the Alps, along the Rhine, in the Apennines, Croatia, the Balkans and Transylvania. Of scattered occurrence on damp, peaty meadows, pastures and fens, also on scree slopes, from the lowlands up to 2,400m (7,800 ft). Prefers limestone, but not confined to it. An annual species, 5 to 30cm (2 in to 12 in) tall, with branching, somewhat angular stems, it forms a basal rosette which withers quite early in the season. The basal leaves are obovate and blunt pointed. The stem leaves are oblong-ovate, with three to five veins. The large, deep azure-blue flowers are carried on lateral and terminal stalks, and the spreading corolla has five pointed lobes. One striking feature is the elongated, inflated, broadly winged calyx.

In the wild it is always a delight to see it, but in the garden it is almost impossible to keep. An attempt may be made by sowing fresh seed in the autumn at the spot where it is hoped to grow it.

Gentiana veitchiorum Hemsl.

A native of western China (Szechuan) and eastern Tibet. After its introduction by E. H. Wilson in 1905 it was distributed under various, now invalid names. In appearance this gentian is much stiffer and more compact than its relatives. It forms basal rosettes with leaves 3.7cm (1½ in) long and up to 6 mm (¼ in) wide, with blunt points. They are dark green above and paler below. Arising from the rosette are spreading shoots or stolons over 10cm (4 in) long. The stem leaves, arranged in pairs round the shoots, are thick and fleshy, and about 1.2cm (½ in) long. The shoots of *G. veitchiorum* have more branches than those of its allies. The flowers are solitary, terminal, and the calyx is 2.5cm (1 in) long with oval-lanceolate lobes half as long as the tube. The corolla is deep royal-blue with broad greenish-yellow stripes on the outside, tubular and up to 5cm (2 in) long. The flowers appear in August and continue into September, when *G. sino ornata* begins to flower. *G. veitchiorum* cannot be confused with related species; in addition to its stiff compact growth, the broader, blunter leaves are a distinguishing mark. The long calyx tube with its short lobes and the long, always tubular corolla are other points for identification.

A good garden plant, though less often seen than the hybrids, it does not grow as vigorously as *G. sino ornata*. It should be cultivated in good, lime-free soil with an adequate supply of moisture. It can be propagated by seed (though this entails some danger of hybridisation), division in spring, or cuttings in early summer.

There is a form named *G. veitchiorum* 'Grandiflorum', which is considerably more vigorous than the original species and has large flowers of brilliant, pure, deep azure-blue. It flowers from August to November and grows to a height of 10cm (4 in). Also in commerce is *G. veitchiorum* 'L.S. 13321', a magnificent plant with dark Oxford-blue flowers. *G. veitchiorum* 'White Seedling' has flowers which are pure-white inside and creamy white outside, appearing from September to October. The species has recently been re-introduced by Reuben Hatch (RH.27) in spectacular forms.

Gentiana venusta (G. Don) Griseb.

A Himalayan plant (Nepal, Kashmir, Kumaon, Sikkim and Pakistan), where it grows on open slopes and peaty soils at altitudes of 3,000 to 4,500m (9,800 to 14,800 ft). It is a small, tufted plant with shoots resembling stolons. The leaves on the non-flowering shoots are broad-spatulate and about 6mm (¼ in) long, while those on the flowering shoots are broader, up to 10mm (⅜ in). The flowering shoots, several in number, are spreading, 2 to 8cm (¾ to 3⅛ in) long, turning upwards near their tips, covered with leaves for their whole length and carrying a

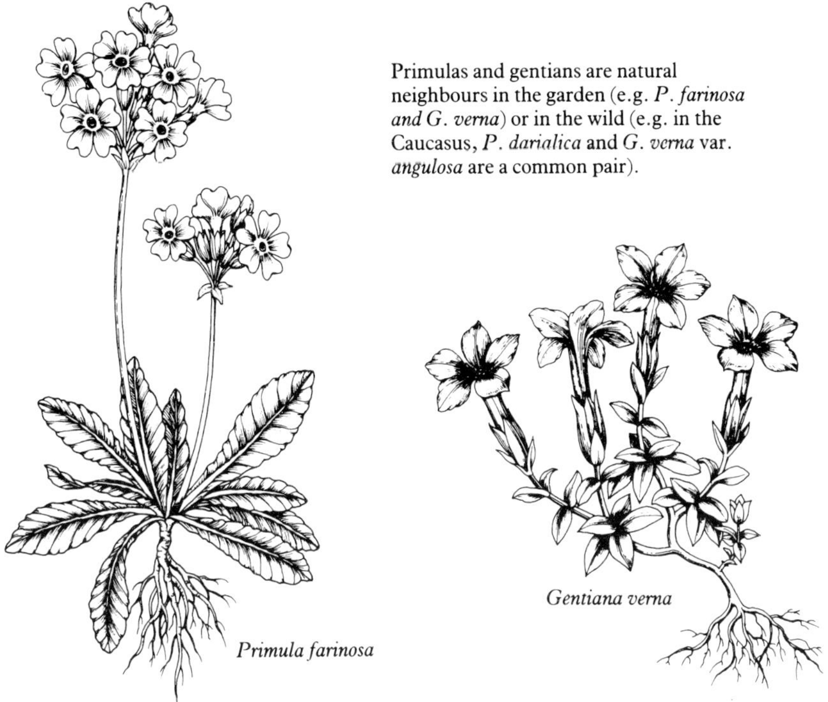

Figure 14 Gentians in association with other plants

single flower. The tubular, blue flowers have rounded, ovate corolla lobes and irregularly toothed plicae. The flowers are 2 to 2.5cm (¾ to 1 in) long, yellowish inside. The calyx is 6mm (¼ in) long with oblong, pointed lobes. In the wild this species flowers in August and September.

Although introduced more than 100 years ago this beautiful species has not proved permanent in cultivation. It requires full sun and stony soil with adequate supplies of moisture during the growing period. It is propagated by seed or cuttings from non-flowering shoots.

Gentiana verna L. (spring gentian)

SYNONYM: *Hippion vernum* (L.) F. W. Schmidt

Found in mountain districts in Spain, central France, the Jura, Pyrenees, Carpathians and Abruzzi, England, Ireland, Norway, central Europe, the Balkans, Asia Minor, the Caucasus, Turkestan, Afghanistan, the Altai, the Baikal district, eastern Siberia and Mongolia. In the

Alps and their foothills it occurs both on limestone and igneous rocks. Of scattered occurrence, usually in colonies, in dry and moist meadows, pastures and heaths, in dwarf shrub heath, on dry banks, on rocks, in fens, in thin woodland and many other places.

As might be expected from its enormous range, a large number of different forms have been described. The species grows in loose mats reaching a height of 3 to 12cm (1 to 5 in). It consists of unbranched shoots, barren or flowering, the latter carrying a single flower or occasionally two or three. The leaves of the basal rosette are elliptic-lanceolate, narrowed at both ends, three veined and roughly twice as long as broad. The short, erect stems lengthen at flowering time and carry two or three pairs of spatulate leaves. The terminal flower has a tubular calyx 1.5 to 2cm (5/8 to 3/4 in) long, with sharply pointed, lanceolate teeth 3 to 6mm (1/8 to 1/4 in) in length. The saucer-shaped flower is normally deep azure-blue, 1.8 to 3cm (3/4 to 1 3/16 in) in diameter, with a narrow tube and ovate corolla lobes 7 to 12mm (1/4 to 1/2 in) long. Besides the more normal, brilliant-blue form, other tints are occasionally seen, including pink, violet and white and their intermediates. A violet-purple form of natural origin is commercially available under the name *G. verna* var. *rubra*. In nature it flowers from May to August. 'Hegi' (*Illustrierte Flora von Mittel-Europa*) lists numerous varieties and forms; *Flora Europaea* reduces the European taxa to three subspecies:

1. *G. verna* ssp. *verna*. Widely distributed throughout most of the range. Leaves usually lanceolate or elliptical, occasionally acute. Wings of calyx 1–2mm (1/32–1/16 in) wide. Corolla lobes obtuse.
2. *G. verna* ssp. *pontica* (Soltok.) Hayek. In the central and eastern parts of the Balkan peninsula. Rosette leaves broadly ovate, about twice as long as wide. Wings of calyx 2–3mm (1/16–1/8 in) wide. Corolla lobes obtuse.
3. *G. verna* ssp. *tergestina* (G. Beck) Hayek (syn. *G. tergestina* Beck). Northern and western parts of the Balkan peninsula, south western Bulgaria, Italy. Rosette leaves narrowly lanceolate, acuminate, about four times as long as wide. Wings of calyx about 4mm (3/16 in) wide. Corolla lobes acute.

This subdivision is mainly of botanical interest. Of much greater importance to gardeners is the Caucasian variety, *G. verna* var. *angulosa* Wahlenb. (syn. *G. angulosa* M.B.). In certain publications the synonym is given preference, but in view of its very close affinity the status of a separate species does not seem justified. The supposition that *G. verna* ssp. *tergestina* is identical with *G. verna* var. *angulosa*, put forward in

Hegi (1927) and elsewhere, is not really tenable and receives no support in *Flora Europaea*. From the gardener's angle it should be noted that the Caucasian variety is much more easily grown than *G. verna* from the Alps. Its flowers are somewhat larger and their colour slightly paler though in general it resembles the type species. The species and its variety can easily be distinguished by examining the calyx: in *G. verna* it is angled or very slightly winged, whereas *G. verna* var. *angulosa* has five distinct wings along the calyx tube extending to the points of the calyx lobes. They can also be distinguished by their leaves: in *G. verna* the leaves are two to three times as long as broad, whereas in *G. verna* var. *angulosa* they are three to four times as long as broad, i.e. more elongated. In the Caucasus it is found on lime-free soils, for example on Mount Elbrus it grows in pockets of humus on a subsoil of volcanic rubble and obsidian. In the plant trials *G. verna* var. *angulosa* received the designation of a perennial for enthusiasts.

Yet another jewel from the Caucasus is the yellow-flowered *G. verna* var. *oschtenica* (Kusn.), (syn. *G. oschtenica* Kusn.). Here again, flower colour alone does not justify its promotion to the dignity of a species. Treasured by plantsmen, it is now in cultivation once more and seed is occasionally offered in the exchanges.

All these *G. verna* types can be propagated by seed, though division and cuttings are also feasible. In the garden they require an open, sunny position with moderate soil moisture, high atmospheric humidity and good drainage. In lowland gardens these conditions are not always easy to meet. Various growing mixtures have been recommended, for example equal parts of river sand, well-rotted cow manure, loam, peat and crushed brick with the addition of a little bone meal. An alternative recipe consists of loam derived from peaty turf, with the addition of sand, finely chopped sphagnum and limestone grit. Other growers recommend frequent sprinklings with finely sieved earth. But Wocke writes that *G. verna* is not happy when grown by itself but requires a close growing community of other plants such as *Primula farinosa* and *Ranunculus alpestris*. Other suitable associates include *Carex firma*, *Carlina acaulis*, *Globularia*, *Phyteuma scheuchzeri* and *Pulsatilla vernalis*. Experience has shown that consistent success can be derived from plants grown in a trough with a freely drained mixture containing loam over a layer of well-rotted manure.

As early as 1613 *G. verna* was listed as *Gentianella minima verna flore coerulea* in the *Hortus Eystettensis*; nevertheless, it would be wrong to claim that it has ever been a success in the garden. It remains an alpine treasure, difficult to keep and suitable only for the enthusiast. It likes moist, peaty loam and full sun. It is propagated by seed, and pot-grown seedlings should be planted out with their root-balls intact. *G. verna* var. *angulosa* is a better garden plant and will flourish under somewhat drier conditions. In the garden it flowers in April or May.

Gentiana villosa L.

SYNONYM: *G. ochroleuca* Froel.

An American species found from Delaware to northern Florida. It has unbranched stems 45cm (18 in) tall with oval leaves 7.5cm (3 in) long. The flowers are carried in terminal clusters; the calyx tube is 1.8cm (¾ in) long with lobes 1cm (⅜ in) long. The corolla is greenish-white, sometimes with a bluish-violet tinge, tubular, and about 3.7cm (1½ in) long. In the wild it does not flower until September to December, and in cold climates it often fails to bloom at all. Propagated by seed, in cultivation it demands moist soil.

Gentiana waltonii Burkhill

A native of Tibet, where it occurs at altitudes of 3,500m (11,400 ft) upwards, mainly on dry, sandy slopes and on sunny rock outcrops. It forms a distinct rosette of linear-lanceolate leaves up to 16cm (6½ in) long and about 1.8cm (¾ in) wide; they have three to five veins and taper at both ends. One or two more or less erect, though mainly prostrate stems, 30cm (12 in) long, arise from these rosettes. The stem leaves have the same shape as the rosette leaves but are only 5cm (2 in) long; they are arranged in pairs, the base of each pair forming a tube round the stem. The flowers are carried singly in the upper leaf axils or in a loose terminal cluster. The terminal flowers are stalkless, the axillary flowers stalked. The calyx tube is split for most of its length. The narrow, bell-shaped corolla is deep blue to purplish-blue (sometimes paler) and about 3.7cm (1½ in) long. The corolla lobes are broad ovate and more than twice as long as the plicae. It flowers in August–September. It is closely related to *G. decumbens*, and both have a split calyx, but in *G. waltonii* the calyx lobes are ovate and acute, whereas in *G. decumbens* the calyx lobes, normally three in number, are very short and awl shaped. The corolla of *G. waltonii* is longer, and it forms a larger plant than *G. decumbens*. In the garden it likes a warm situation and stony soil.

Gentiana walujewii Regel et Schmalh.

The only variety grown in gardens is *G. walujewii* var. *kesselringii* (Regel) Kusn. (syn. *G. kesselringii* Regel) from the high mountains of eastern Turkestan. It forms a basal rosette consisting of linear-lanceolate leaves 7 to 15cm (3 to 6 in) long, with three to five veins and sharp points. The sprawling stems, 20 to 30cm (8 to 12 in) long, carry three or four pairs of stem leaves; these are smaller than the basal leaves and broad lanceolate; at their base they form a tube which clasps the stem. The uppermost stem leaves surround the terminal flowers like bracts. The flowers are whitish with scattered dots of blue or bluish-purple. The corolla is twice as long as the unsplit calyx; in shape it is tubular with a thickening above the middle. It flowers in July or August. The whitish colour of the flowers distinguishes the species from its close relatives such as *G. decumbens* or *G. olivieri*.

In cultivation it presents no difficulty provided it has good drainage and sufficient sunlight. Propagation is by seed. Not an outstanding beauty, but a plant for collectors and enthusiasts.

Gentiana yakushimensis Makino

In catalogues this species is sometimes incorrectly listed as *G. yakusimana*.

It comes from Japan, where it is a native of the mountains of the southernmost highlands, and unlike most other Japanese species it grows on limestone. It forms long, thick, fleshy roots deeply anchored in the rock, and reaches a height of 4 to 25cm (1⅝ to 10 in) depending on the conditions in which it grows. The leaves are deep green above and almost whitish below. The long, blue solitary flowers appear in August. It is propagated by seed.

Not yet widespread in cultivation, it does not like full sun. It requires gritty soil rich in humus with good drainage but adequate moisture during the growing period.

The less common and less important species

This section comprises species seldom or never seen in gardens, short-lived species of only one or two years' duration, and lastly species from warmer latitudes which require protection in an alpine house or cold house. As a consequence of the growing ease of worldwide travel, and through the seed lists put out by botanical gardens and horticultural societies, the enthusiast may encounter some of the less common species and may have an opportunity of growing gentians which have never before appeared in cultivation. Even among the short-lived species there are some beautiful plants.

Some species can be propagated comparatively easily by sowing the seed at the spot where the plants are required to grow and exposing it to snow and low temperatures. Other species, including those from New Zealand, Formosa and New Guinea, must be grown in frames or greenhouses, since they cannot tolerate temperatures much below zero.

Gentiana aquatica L.

SYNONYMS: *G. prostrata* Boiss. (non Haenke nec Gross), *G. fremontii* Tort., *G. humilis* Stev., *Chondrophylla fremontii* (Torr.) A. Nels.

Widely distributed in North America and Asia (Himalayas), it grows in wet meadows and at the margins of bogs. A small, annual or biennial plant, normally branching from the base, and 3 to 10cm ($1\frac{3}{16}$ to 4 in) tall. The numerous leaves are less than 6mm ($\frac{1}{4}$ in) long, the basal leaves being obovate and the upper leaves linear–lanceolate. Small, solitary, purplish-green flowers, 5 to 8mm ($\frac{3}{16}$ to $\frac{5}{16}$ in) long, appear at the ends of the stems and it is of no garden value.

G. aquatica var. *karelinii* Clarke (syn. *G. karelinii* Griseb.) is a variety found mainly in Siberia (Badakhschan), and also in Ladakh at altitudes of 3,400 to 4,200m (11,200 to 13,800 ft) where it grows among sedges on mountain pastures. A biennial plant 3 to 12cm ($1\frac{3}{16}$ to 5 in) tall with two to four blue to light-blue flowers 14 to 20mm ($\frac{9}{16}$ to $\frac{15}{16}$ in) long which appear in June–July. It is fully hardy in central Europe.

Gentiana arctophila Griseb.

Found in the arctic-alpine regions of north-western America where it grows on dry, sunny slopes. A dwarf plant, annual or biennial, it has a narrow rosette of obovate sessile leaves from which arise one or more stems 5 to 15cm (2 to 6 in) tall carrying one or more flowers. The corolla is about 1.5 to 2.5cm ($\frac{5}{8}$ to 1 in) long, deep blue with triangular or ovate lobes.

Gentiana argentea (D. Don) C. B. Clarke

Found in Pakistan and Nepal on open scrub-covered slopes at altitudes of 2,100 to 4,300m (6,800 to 14,100 ft). A delicate annual, 2.5 to 10cm (1 to 4 in) tall, conspicuous because of its brilliant, silvery, slightly reflexed and slightly pointed leaves. The small, blue terminal flowers are about 8mm ($\frac{5}{16}$ in) long.

Gentiana arisanensis Hayata

SYNONYM: *G. caespitosa* Hayata

From the mountains of Taiwan on rocks and turf, 2,300 to 3,900m (7,500 to 12,800 ft). A small tufted plant with unbranched stems 3 to 13cm (1 to 5 in) tall and small oval opposite entire leaves 5 to 6mm (3/16 in) long and solitary terminal starry broad, bell-shaped blue flowers. A recent set of postage stamps of high alpine plants from Taiwan depicts this species, though its flowers appear rose-pink rather than blue.

Gentiana armerioides Griseb.

A South American species which grows in rocky places. It forms dense clumps 5 to 6cm (2 to 2 3/8 in) tall and 7 to 8cm (2 3/4 to 3 3/16 in) wide with red or yellow flowers. The numerous non-flowering shoots have fleshy spoon-shaped leaves. Still rare in cultivation.

Gentiana atkinsonii Burkhill

Found on the island of Taiwan on grasslands at altitudes from 2,400 to 3,200m (7,900 to 10,500 ft). One special form confined to the island is *G. atkinsonii* Burkhill var. *formosana* (Hayata) Yamamoto. A low-growing perennial, 5 to 20cm (2 to 8 in) tall, with paired sessile leaves. Basal leaves close set, 3 to 7cm (1 3/16 to 2 3/4 in) long. Flowers solitary or in clusters of two to five at the top of the stem, blue or light blue, bell shaped to tubular, 1.5 to 2.5cm (5/8 to 1 in) long.

Gentiana auriculata (Pall.) Vaut.

SYNONYM: *G. fauriei* Lev. et Vaut.

Hokkaido (Japan), Sakhalin, Kurile and Aleutian Islands, northern Asia. A biennial species, 5 to 20cm (2 to 8 in) in height, with unbranched or scantily branched stems carrying blue flowers 2.5 to 3cm (1 to 1 3/16 in) long.

Gentiana boryi Boiss.

Spain (Sierra Nevada, Sierra de Gredos, Cantabrian Cordilleras) on moist hillsides from 900 to 3,000m (3,000 to 9,800 ft). A low, tufted perennial, 2 to 5cm (3/4 to 2 in) high. Stems erect, unbranched, leaves ovate to semi-circular, blunt at the tips, of thick consistency. Calyx lobes ovate with a long point, flowers 8 to 10mm (5/16 to 3/8 in) long, obconical, the upper surfaces of the lobes blue, the exterior, dark, bluish-green with white plicae and a light-blue appendage at the sinus. Similar to *G. pyrenaica*, but even more difficult in cultivation.

Gentiana capitata Buch.-Ham. ex Don

From Pakistan to south-eastern Tibet in woods and scrub at altitudes between 1,500 and 4,500m (5,000 and 14,800 ft). A plant only 2 to 10cm (¾ to 4 in) tall, easily recognisable by its slightly oval leaves, borne in closed tufts below the flowers, while the lower part of the stem is usually leafless. The flowers are blue or white and about 6mm (¼ in) long. Flowering time December to April, depending on altitude.

Gentiana carinata Griseb.

Pakistan, Kashmir, on open slopes at altitudes of 3,000 to 4,300m (9,800 to 14,100 ft). A small annual species, only 2 to 5cm (¾ to 2 in) tall, with dark-blue flowers.

Gentiana catesbaei Walt.

SYNONYM: *G. elliottii* Chapm. not Raf., *G. parvifolia* (Chapm.) Britt.

Through North America from Delaware to Alaska. Up to 60cm (24 in) tall, leaves ovate-lanceolate up to 5cm (2 in) long. Small numbers of blue flowers, 1cm (⅜ in) long, grouped in a tufted terminal inflorescence.

Gentiana cerina Hook f.

This species, together with *G. cerina* var. *suberecta*, is confined to the Auckland Islands. Dwarf plants with broad, bell-shaped white flowers, striped or spotted with red or violet; also some of pure violet colour.

Gentiana chrysotaenia Gilg.

A beautiful species from South America, 7 to 10cm (2¾ to 4 in) tall (otherwise given as 2.5 to 4cm (1 to 1⅝ in). A perennial with fire-red flowers striped with yellow. Lime tolerant. Has recently appeared in seed lists but as yet hardly seen in cultivation.

Gentiana clarkei Kusn.

SYNONYM: *G. pygmaea* Clarke

Siberia (Badakhshan), Kashmir and other parts of the Himalaya in moist, sedgy meadows at altitudes from 4,100 to 4,300m (13,500 to 14,100 ft). An annual species, 8 to 13cm (3 3/16 to 5⅛ in) tall with solitary, pale-blue or blue flowers.

Gentiana cruttwellii H. Smith

This species from New Guinea is 15cm (6 in) tall with purple-tinged stems carrying blue flowers of varied hues, darker externally, sometimes with greenish bands.

Gentiana dilatata Griseb.

SYNONYM: *G. primulaefolia* Griseb.

A South American plant of moist places. Up to about 10cm (4 in) tall with fleshy leaves and greenish flowers with violet corolla lobes. Seldom seen in cultivation.

Gentiana douglasiana Bong.

From the coastal districts and offshore islands of Alaska and British Columbia. An annual with numerous flowers measuring about 1.2cm (½ in) with a greenish corolla tube and blue or purplish-blue lobes. There are also white forms.

Gentiana ettinghausenii

Widely distributed in the mountains of Papua New Guinea where it occurs at altitudes of 1,800 to 2,000m (5,900 to 6,500 ft) (Mount Suckling). On Mount Wilhelm it reaches 4,328m (14,200 ft). Plants growing at higher altitudes are more compact and have larger flowers. In appearance it is intermediate between *G. cruttwellii* and *G. juniperina*. The short, reddish stems carry opposite, more or less linear, sharply pointed leaves. The stems are branched and have up to three flowers, 2cm (¾ in) or more in diameter. In colour they are a brilliant sky-blue with a dark throat. As in most of these species, the flowers open only in full sun.

Gentiana flavo-maculata Hayata

From high mountains in Taiwan (Formosa), chiefly on rocks at 2,000 to 4,300m (6,500 to 14,100 ft). A perennial 4 to 10cm (1⅝ to 4 in) tall with slender, branching stems and solitary, terminal yellow flowers with scattered black dots at the base. The corolla is bell shaped and 1.2 to 1.5cm (½ to ⅝ in) long.

Gentiana gibbsii Petrie.

From the South Island of New Zealand, in the lowlands and subalpine zone up to 900m (2,900 ft), in grassy pastures and marshy areas among other perennials. Arising from the basal leaves are several stems, 6 to 15cm ($2\frac{3}{8}$ to 6 in) tall, carrying small numbers of stem leaves. The solitary, terminal flowers are of elongated form with a white corolla and long, pointed calyx lobes (equal in length to the corolla).

Gentiana grisebachii Hook f.

North and South Islands of New Zealand at altitudes around 1,400m (4,600 ft), at the treeline, on moist, grassy pastures and among other perennials. Solitary or paired, terminal white flowers on slender stems 7 to 20cm ($2\frac{3}{4}$ to 8 in) tall. The calyx and corolla have deeply cut lobes.

Gentiana hypericoides Gilg.

A shrubby plant from South America, 15 to 40cm (6 to 16 in) tall with leathery leaves. The corolla is 3 to 5cm ($1\frac{3}{16}$ to 2 in) long, of velvety texture and carmine-red colour. An unusual plant. A native of warmer regions and presumably unsuited for temperate-zone gardens.

Gentiana igittii van Royen

From New Guinea, where it grows in grass on peaty soil and forms tufted plants about 13cm ($5\frac{1}{8}$ in) tall with pale, bluish-violet or pale-blue flowers with a violet tube.

Gentiana incurva Hook.

South America. A low-growing perennial with strongly developed roots and cup-shaped, sulphur-yellow flowers, their margins often tinged with scarlet. It forms a basal rosette and grows to a height of 10cm (4 in) or more. Seldom seen in cultivation.

Gentiana juniperina H. Smith

From New Guinea, where it grows on open grassy slopes. About 13 to 15cm ($5\frac{1}{8}$ to 6 in) tall. The flowers are dark blue on the exterior and white in the interior, with dark spots.

Gentiana leucomelaena Maxim.

Pamir, altitude 2,700 to 3,500m (8,800 to 11,400 ft). A biennial, 1 to 10cm ($\frac{3}{8}$ to 4 in) tall. Flowers dull white, pale blue or blue, 8 to 20mm ($\frac{5}{16}$ to $\frac{3}{4}$ in) in diameter. Leaves mottled with white.

Gentiana lineata Kirh.

On the South Island of New Zealand in boggy scrubland at low altitudes and in the subalpine zone up to 1,100m (3,600 ft). A curious, much branched species, 5 to 10cm (2 to 4 in) tall and 10cm (4 in) broad, with interlacing stems. Numerous, small basal leaves and even smaller stem leaves. Small, solitary, terminal, white flowers. Deeply cut calyx with pointed calyx lobes.

Found chiefly on Stewart Island on grassland, where it is not too dry—in the alpine and subalpine zones, also among low shrubs, on rocks and river flood zones. In the wild in New Zealand it flowers from November to February.

Gentiana marginata (G. Don) Griseb.

From Afghanistan and Pakistan on open hillsides at 2,700 to 4,300m (8,800 to 14,100 ft). Resembles *G. carinata*; an annual, up to 5cm (2 in) tall, with pale-blue flowers.

Gentiana matthewsii Petrie

New Zealand, subalpine zone from 800 to 1,300m (2,600 to 4,300 ft). Occurs chiefly on level patches saturated with snowmelt water where non-woody plants grow, and on grassy areas near the treeline. Similar to *G. grisebachii* but more robust and upright, up to 25cm (10 in) tall. Has a few basal leaves and smaller stem leaves, which are sessile and clasp the stem. Flowers solitary or in pairs, white.

Gentiana melandrifolia Franch.

A native of China (Cang Shan range), recently introduced into cultivation. Rising from a central rosette of diamond-shaped leaves are the spreading stems, 10 to 15cm (4 to 6 in) long, each carrying a terminal tuft of tubular blue flowers. Requires a sheltered shady place if it is to flourish.

Gentiana montana Forst. f.

New Zealand, South Island, subalpine and low alpine zones between 500 and 1,500m (1,600 and 5,000 ft). Grows in moist turf in places where there is high precipitation and also in patches of sphagnum. Has a basal rosette of leathery, dark-green leaves 1.5 to 2cm (⅝ to ¾ in) long. Stems robust, usually single, 10 to 40cm (4 to 16 in) or up to 60cm (24 in) tall. The basal rosette is sometimes absent. The branching stems carry a racemose inflorescence with up to ten white flowers. *G. montana* var. *stolonifera* Cheesem. is more slender and has stems 10 to 15cm (4 to 6 in) long which tend to be prostrate or creeping; flowers less numerous. Both kinds flower in late summer.

G. montana forms rounded clumps up to 50cm (20 in) in diameter, and its large flowers, up to 2.5cm (1 in) resemble those of *G. corymbifera*, but the flowering stems are more thickly clothed with leaves than in the latter species.

Gentiana nivalis L. (snow gentian)

In the southern and eastern Alps, on meadows, pastures and heaths, in thin woodland and marshes, on both limestone and igneous rocks, 1,900 to 2,700m (6,200 to 8,800 ft). Also found in many other mountain ranges, including the Pyrenees, Carpathians, Abruzzi, Jura, Balkans, Asia Minor, Greenland, Arctic North America and Scotland. An annual, 2 to 15cm (¾ to 6 in) tall, stems simple or branched with a basal rosette of pale-green, lanceolate leaves. The brilliant-blue flowers are 12 to 18mm (½ to ¾ in) in diameter. Calyx tube angled and slightly inflated. The flowers open only in sunshine. Hardly ever seen in gardens.

Gentiana olgae Regel et Schmalh.

Occurs in the central part of the Turkestan mountains (Kusalsi-Sai to 2,800m (9,200 ft)). Found chiefly on mountain meadows of steppe-like character but also in somewhat moister places. There it is associated with *Ranunculus trautvetterianus*, *Corydalis nudicaulis*, *Gagea hissarica*, *Paraquilegia uniflora*, *Colchicum luteum* and *Anemone protracta*. The plants are only 10 to 15cm (4 to 6 in) tall and have bluish-violet flowers. Has recently been grown from seed by a few enthusiasts.

Gentiana papuiana van Royen

New Guinea. A cushion-forming species about 5cm (2 in) tall; blue flowers with a white throat.

Gentiana parvifolia Hayata

From mountainous districts in the north and south of Taiwan, at altitudes of 2,600 to 3,100m (8,500 to 10,100 ft), chiefly in woodland. A perennial with spreading stems 15 to 35cm (6 to 14 in) long. The stem leaves are ovate or ovate-lanceolate, 1.5 to 2cm (about ¾ in) long, with pointed tips. Flowers solitary or in twos, terminal or in the leaf axils, bell shaped, wide open at the mouth, 2.2 to 2.6cm (about 1 in) long. Yellowish-white.

Gentiana patula (Kirk) Cheesem.

New Zealand, North Island and South Island, in mountainous country at 400 to 1,200m (1,300 to 3,900 ft), in moist, grassy places. A plant up to 20cm (8 in) tall, similar in many respects to *G. bellidifolia*. Flowers white, often veined with violet; basal leaves larger than those of *G. bellidifolia*. Sometimes puts out underground stolons.

Gentiana pedicellata (D. Don) Griseb.

SYNONYM: *G. heterostemon* H. Smith

Pakistan to Bhutan. An annual, sometimes occurring on cultivated ground at lower altitudes. Up to 8cm (3³⁄16 in) tall, though usually shorter, with pale-blue flowers.

Gentiana phyllocalyx C. B. Clarke

Central Nepal to south western China on open hillsides among dwarf rhododendrons at altitudes of 3,600 to 5,500m (11,800 to 18,000 ft). Height 2 to 10cm (¾ to 4 in) basal leaves broad ovate to rounded, approx. 2cm (¾ in) long, forming a rosette; the upper stem leaves clasp the base of the corolla. All the leaves are thick and fleshy. Flowers are pale blue to deep blue with erect, triangular corolla lobes. Flowering time June–August.

Gentiana propinqua Richards

Newfoundland, Hudson Bay, Alberta, British Columbia, Yukon, Alaska and north-eastern Asia, on dry, sunny hillsides. Annual or biennial. Resembles *G. arctophila*, but the stems are 10 to 25cm (4 to 10 in) tall, often more slender, flowers smaller. Branches from the axils of the upper stem leaves.

Gentiana prostrata Haenke

SYNONYM: *G. nutans* Hunge

Eastern Alps, northern and arctic Siberia, southwards as far as Turkestan, also north-eastern Tibet, north-western America, South America, in the Andes. Scattered occurrence in damp, stony, short grass, on igneous rock and limestone, at 2,200 to 2,800m (7,200 to 9,200 ft). An annual species of variable appearance, about 5cm (2 in) tall, hairless, without non-flowering shoots. Stems simple or with a few basal branches, spreading or upright. Flowers solitary, terminal, in four or five parts; long calyx and funnel-shaped or tubular corolla, steel blue, greenish-white at the base. Of no garden value.

Gentiana pterocalyx Franch. ex. F. Forbes et Hemsl.

Yunnan. A branching annual plant, 30cm (12 in) or taller, with oval, heart-shaped leaves about 2.5cm (1 in) long. Flowers deep sky-blue to yellowish, about 5cm (2 in) long.

Gentiana puendensis

Mountains of Papua New Guinea. Forms dense spreading mats of dark-green, needle-shaped leaves, flushed whitish on the lower surfaces. The four petalled flowers are pale blue. A rare endemic.

Gentiana purdomii Marq.

From China (Kansu), this species is seldom if ever seen in cultivation; the plants grown in gardens under this name are *G. gracilipes* or *G. dahurica*. Erect stems about 20cm (8 in) tall, basal leaves linear-lanceolate up to 15cm (6 in) long, stem leaves 2.5 cm (1 in) long with a distinct sheath. Flowers in terminal clusters of six to eight surrounded by leaves. Flowers stalked, 2.5cm (1 in) or more long, yellowish with purple stripes.

Gentiana quadrifaria *Blume.*

Java. A small perennial with a tap root. Leaves ovate to elliptic-obovate, about 1cm (3⁄8 in) long. Flowers tubular-bell shaped, dark blue, about 1cm (3⁄8 in) long. Calyx about 6mm (1⁄4 in), divided to the middle.

Gentiana regina Gilg.

A South American species up to 1cm (3⁄8 in) tall with bell-shaped violet flowers. In the wild it grows on limestone subsoils. Not yet in cultivation.

Gentiana rochellii A. Kern.

Hungary. Probably no more than a Hungarian variant of *G. clusii* with stems 5 to 7.5cm (2 to 3 in) tall. Leaves at the base grouped into a rounded cluster, about 3.8cm (1½ in) long. Flowers blue, over 5cm (2 in) long.

Gentiana scabrida Hayata

Mountains of Taiwan from 2,220 to 3,100m (7,200 to 10,100 ft). An annual species, 15 to 20cm (6 to 8 in) tall, with whitish or yellowish flowers. Also *G. scabrida* var. *punctulata* Ying, with pale-yellow flowers thickly dotted with black spots at the base.

Gentiana scarlatina Gilg.

A little-known South American species, only 4 to 7cm (1⅝ to 2¾ in) tall. Like many South American gentians it has red flowers.

Gentiana scarlatino-striata Gilg.

A beautiful and unmistakable South American species with rosettes of oblong-lanceolate, pointed, fleshy leaves and several flowering stems about 15cm (6 in) tall. These carry pendant, bell-shaped, red flowers striped with yellow in a pseudoraceme.

Gentiana spenceri Kirk

South Island of New Zealand at subalpine and low alpine altitudes from 900 to 1,600m (2,900 to 5,200 ft), growing among herbaceous plants irrigated by snowmelt water, and also in scrubland and thin woodland. In habit and flowers closely similar to *G. montana*, yet comparatively easily distinguished by its inflorescence. Flower colour is white.

Gentiana stipitata Edgew.

Nepal, Pakistan, on stony mountainsides at 3,600 to 4,500m (11,800 to 14,800 ft). A small plant forming tufts 5cm (2 in) tall consisting of a few short shoots. Flowers tubular, up to 2.5cm (1 in) long with pointed corolla lobes, pale mauve with a greenish interior, often marked with dark lines. Leaves small, elliptical, opposite, 1 to 2cm (⅜ to ¾ in) long and 0.5 to 1cm (about ¼ in) wide.

Gentiana stracheyi (Clarke) Kita.

SYNONYM: *G. detonsa* Fries. var. *stracheyi* Clarke ex Hook.

In the mountains between Kashmir and Ladakh. An erect perennial with leaves 3 to 5cm (1³⁄₁₆ to 2 in) wide. The flowering shoots are 5 to 15cm (2 to 6in) long, calyx tube 1 to 1.5cm (⅜ to ⅝ in), stout, with four ribs. The blue corolla is fringed at its edges. Conspicuous glands at the base. Flowers from July to September.

Gentiana takedae Kitag.

Japan. A rare annual or biennial species 5 to 25cm (2 to 10 in) tall; flowers pale purplish-blue, 1.6 to 2.2cm (5/8 to 7/8 in) long, corolla lobes whitish.

Gentiana thunbergii (G. Don) Griseb.

Japan, Korea, Manchuria, China. An annual or biennial, rosette-forming species. Basal leaves oval, about 3.8cm (1½ in) long, with translucent margins; stem leaves shorter and narrower. Flowers terminal, stalked, calyx half as long as corolla (approx. 2.8cm (1⅛ in) long), blue. *G. thunbergii* var. *minor* Maxim., reported from Japan, has smaller, paler flowers.

Gentiana tongolensis Franch.

Western China. An annual species with oblong-oval basal leaves. The stem leaves are oblong-lanceolate. Flowers terminal, yellow, about 5cm (2 in) long, narrow tubular.

Gentiana urnula Harry Smith

Occurs from eastern Nepal to south-eastern Tibet at altitudes of 4,500 to over 6,000m (14,800 to over 19,700 ft), on rocks and screes. Forms mats and clumps with stunning grey-blue flowers 2.5cm (1 in) long. Easily recognisable by the oval, overlapping leaves. Flowers in September–October.

Gentiana vernicosa Cheesem.

South Island of New Zealand at subalpine altitudes from 1,200 to 15,000m (3,900 to 4,900 ft) among low-growing perennials irrigated by snowmelt water. The plants are about 10cm (4 in) tall and wide, with one to five creeping stems terminating in upright leafy shoots. The leaves are thick, narrow and pointed; flowers white, in terminal clusters of one to seven.

Gentiana yuparensis Takeda

SYNONYMS: *G. yezoalpina* Koidz., *G. yuparensis* var. *yezoalpina* (Koidz.) Kudo

An alpine plant from Japan. A biennial species, 10 to 20cm (4 to 8 in) tall with obovate basal leaves and whitish flowers.

Gentiana zollingeri Fawc.

Japan. Annual or biennial, 15cm (6 in) tall, leaves ovate, up to 1.2cm (½ in) long. Flowers in terminal clusters of one to three, tubular; calyx 6mm (¼ in) long; corolla 2.5cm (1 in) long, blue, sometimes tinged with purple.

Gentian hybrids

In large and wide-ranging genera such as *Gentiana* the emergence of hybrids is to be expected, both from chance crossings in the wild and from the activities of plant breeders. In the wild two conditions must be fulfilled: the areas occupied by the parent species must touch or overlap, and their relationship must be close enough for the chromosomes to correspond.

Natural hybrids are particularly numerous in Section Coelanthe (Kusnezow's classification) eg:

Gentiana lutea L. × *G. purpurea* L. = *G.* × *hybrida* Schleich. nec Vill.

G. L. × *G. punctata* L. = *G.* × *doerfleri* Ronn.

Gentiana lutea L. × *G. pannonica* Scop. = *G.* × *haengstii* Hausmann

G. purpurea L. × *G. punctata* L. = *G.* × *spuria* Lebert

G. purpurea L. × *G. pannonica* Scop. = *Gentiana* × *kusnezowiana* Ronn.

This last crossing took place in a garden, not in the wild.

G. × *marcailhouana* Rouy (*G. burseri* × *G. lutea*) is a noteworthy plant which occurs in the Pyrenees. A specimen found by Wilhelm Schacht, one of the great alpine plantsmen, was established in the wild alpine garden of the Botanical Garden at Munich-Nymphenburg and developed into a magnificent plant. The hybrid can be identified by its flower colour and leaf shape. In the older literature this cross is sometimes referred to as *G.* × *burserlutea*.

In Section Cyclostigma the natural hybrid *G.* × *ambigua* Hayek has been recorded (*G. brachyphylla* Vill. × *G. verna* L.). One noteworthy garden hybrid is *G. verna* × *G. pumila*, a plant about 7cm (2¾ in) tall, producing pure blue flowers with white stamens in May–June; it is a plant for the specialist rather than the ordinary grower. A cross between

G. verna × *G. acaulis* appeared at the nurseries of Eschmann, Emmen (Switzerland); it grows to a height of about 10cm (4 in) and carries brilliant, pure, azure-blue flowers in May–June.

In Section Thylactis there is a natural hybrid *G.* × *digenea* Jak. (*G. clusii* Perr. et Song. × *G. acaulis* L.). The natural hybrids of European gentian species are not of much garden value.

Autumn-flowering gentian hybrids

The introduction of the Asiatic autumn-flowering gentians in the early decades of this century was soon followed by the emergence of the first hybrids—chiefly in Great Britain. The species themselves are magnificent plants, yet some of the garden hybrids represent an even further advance. The continuing activity of plant breeders in this field has been rewarded by the new hybrids which have recently come from Great Britain, Switzerland, Holland and West Germany. They are of such great value and significance that it seems worthwhile to list them all in alphabetical order. The reader may be confused by the differing nomenclatures. To name the first cross, the specific names of the two parents are joined to make a new name, e.g., *Gentiana* × *'Hexa-farreri'* from *G. hexaphylla* × *G. farreri*. Selections from such crosses, F_2 hybrids and chance seedlings are then given varietal names. The photographic reproduction of blue tints always presents difficulties and the reader is asked to make allowances; furthermore the names employed to describe the colours are inevitably inexact and fanciful. Words such as gentian blue, ultramarine blue, spectral blue, kingfisher blue, Prussian blue, butterfly blue, lobelia blue, oriental blue, cobalt blue, French blue and budgerigar blue can never be more than a vague approximation to the actual colour.

'Admiral' A selection from *Gentiana* × *macaulayi* from Eschmann's nursery in Switzerland, with numerous medium-sized flowers, in colour intense azure-blue with a white throat. Flowering time July–September. About 10cm (4 in) high, vigorous.

'Alpha' This cultivar from Jack Drake's nursery in Scotland originated from a *G.* × *'Hexa-farreri'* selection and flowers in September–October. The brilliant-blue, green-speckled flowers are large and well formed, with a white throat. Floriferous, vigorous and easily propagated, 8cm (3³⁄16 in) tall.

'Apollo' ('Inverleigh' × *G. ornata*) A variety raised in England (H. Bawden). The deep Cambridge-blue flowers are held well above the leafy shoots. A vigorous grower.

'Azurhimmel' Bred by Walter Löw, Weiden. Of outstanding size and beauty. Flowers of elegant shape and impressive size; the colour is a brilliant ultramarine-blue with vivid stripes. Notably healthy and strong growing. In cold districts it should be covered with pine branches for winter protection.

'Bernardii' *G.* × *stevenagensis* 'Bernardii'. Somewhat tubular flowers, dark azure-blue with red stippling and yellow stripes on the exterior. Flowering time August–October. An outstandingly vigorous grower, easily propagated by division. Height about 8cm (3³⁄16 in).

'Blaue Grotte' (× *G. veitchiorum*) from Eschmann in Switzerland. Deep azure-blue with a purplish cast, flowering July–October, 7 to 8cm (2¾ to 3³⁄16 in) tall; more vigorous than its parent.

'Blauer Dom' (× 'Inverleith') from Eschmann in Switzerland, pure ultramarine-blue, medium-sized flowers with deeply indented corolla lobes. One of the earliest flowering varieties in this shade of blue.

'Blue Dusk' A novelty with large flowers of dark azure-blue. Height 12cm (4¾ in), flowering time August–October.

'Blauer Gnom' (× *G. veitchiorum*) from Eschmann in Switzerland. Forms very low, firm cushions with dainty brilliant azure-blue flowers. Long flowering time from July to October; height about 6cm (2⅜ in).

'Blue Bird' An early-flowering cultivar raised by Eschmann in Switzerland with pure dark azure-blue flowers of moderate size. Height about 8cm (3³⁄16 in), flowers in August–September.

'Blue Emperor' from Eschmann in Switzerland has medium-sized flowers of brilliant ultramarine-blue with white throats. About 8cm (3³⁄16 in) tall, flowering time August–October.

'Blue Flame' ('Inverleith' hybrid) Large, bell-shaped flowers of deep azure-blue; about 10cm (4 in) tall, flowering August–October. Raised by Eschmann in Switzerland.

Figure 15 The requirements of Asiatic gentian hybrids

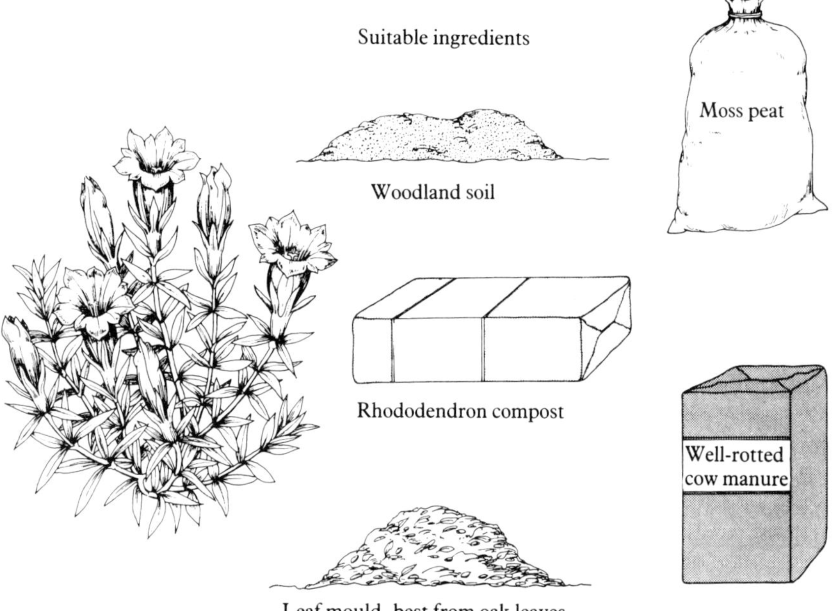

Asiatic autumn-flowering gentian hybrids require specially prepared composts if they are to be grown in districts with alkaline (basic) soil.

'Blue Heaven' Raised by Jack Drake in Scotland. Medium-sized deep-blue flowers; 8cm (3³⁄16 in) tall, flowering August–October.

'Blue King' Raised by Eschmann in Switzerland. An 'Inverleith' seedling with medium-sized flowers of brilliant, pure sapphire-blue. Vigorous, about 10cm (4 in) tall, flowers July–October.

'Caroli' (*G. farreri* × *G. lawrencei*) Early and long flowering; July–October. The colour is described as light enamel-blue, or in other catalogues as deep, copper-sulphate blue. Only 5 to 6cm (2 to 2⅜ in) tall, but very vigorous and easily propagated, since shoots lying on the ground root readily.

'Caroli Azurea' Similar to 'Caroli' but somewhat larger and later flowering; azure blue with a white throat. A charming, early-flowering variety, often producing its first flowers in June; suitable for troughs and sinks.

'Christine Jean' Medium-sized flowers of violet-purple colour in September–October.

'Coronation' (*G. farreri* × *G. veitchiorum*) Of stocky growth forming uniform cushions about 10cm (4 in) high. Narrow leaves resembling those of *G. farreri*. Flowers medium sized, of pure, deep royal-blue with fine dark spots in the interior. Flowers abundantly from July to October. Easily divided.

'Davidii' (*G. prolata* × *G. lawrencei*) Pale sky-blue flowers on branching stems, only just over 4cm (1⅝ in) tall, flowering in September –October.

'Dark Blue Perfection' Raised by Eschmann in Switzerland from *G. veitchiorum* × *G. sino ornata*. Ultramarine blue with a white throat tube marked with dark stripes and dots internally; about 10cm (4 in) tall, flowers August–October.

'Delft' A selected form from Hermann Fuchs, Hof, Germany. Outstandingly large flowers giving an overall impression of Delft ceramic tiles. The interior of the flower is white and the corolla lobes are edged with sky-blue. An impressive plant, flowering at the same time as *Gentiana farreri*.

'Devonhall' (*G. ornata* × *G. farreri*) A good, compact plant with flowers about 5cm (2 in) long appearing in August–September. Colour light blue with a paler throat with greenish spots.

'Diamant' (*G. farreri* × *G. sino ornata*) A variety widely grown in East Germany, selected from numerous seedlings. Cobalt blue, long flowering, very vigorous.

'Drake's Strain' (*G. farreri* × *G. ornata*) raised by Jack Drake in Scotland, 5 to 7cm (2 to 2¾ in) tall, flowering in early autumn. The Cambridge-blue colour is of particular intensity, enhanced by the white throat.

'Drake's Strain White'. Also from Jack Drake, a small-flowered variant of the previous strain, 5 to 6cm (2 to 2⅜ in) tall, with white flowers having a lilac sheen and pencillings in the interior.

'Edina' (*G. ornata* × *G. prolata*) Similar in shape to the female parent (*G. ornata*) but of darker blue. Usually carries several flowers at the end of each stem.

'Elisabeth Brand' A selection from *G.* 'Macaulayi' Similar in appearance to *G.* 'Inverleith'. Flowers 5cm (2 in) long and 3.5cm (1⅜ in) in diameter. Colour described as kingfisher blue. Stems relatively short and tinged with brown.

'Elisabeth Eschmann' (*G. hexaphylla* × *G. farreri*) Early flowering from August–October. Pale azure-blue colour with a reddish sheen. Throat white with dots; about 8 to 10cm (3³⁄16 to 4 in) tall. Raised by Eschmann in Switzerland.

'Emmen' One of the large number of hybrids raised by Eschmann in Switzerland. A typical autumn-flowering plant bearing brilliant butterfly-blue flowers with a white throat. A long-lived perennial. Height 12cm (4¾ in), with large flowers and a long flowering season.

'Excelsior' This has the largest flowers of all the varieties produced by Eschmann in Switzerland, and also has a very long flowering season. Height 15cm (6 in), length of flower tube 8cm (3³⁄16 in), corolla diameter 6cm (2⅜ in). Flowers from August to November. Colour is brilliant ultramarine-blue with a white throat and deeper stripes on the exterior.

'Exploi' Raised by Eschmann in Switzerland. In appearance it resembles a large-flowered *G. veitchiorum*, 12cm (4¾ in) tall, brilliant dark-blue flowers with a white throat, in September–October.

'Farorna' (*G. farreri* × *G. ornata*) Raised from the same cross as 'Devonhall', but the other way round. Closer in overall appearance to *G. ornata* than to *G. farreri*. Flowers of intermediate butterfly-blue with a white or creamy-white corolla, marked with parallel greenish lines on the exterior. Some variation between plants of different origins.

'Fasta Highlands' (also known as *G.* × *fasta* 'Highlands') derived from *G. farreri* × *G.* × *stevenagensis*. A very vigorous grower with large, pure sky-blue flowers with white throats. Late flowering (September–October). About 12cm (4¾ in) tall with long, pointed, needle-shaped leaves.

'Glendevon' (*G. ornata* × *G. sino ornata*) 5 to 6cm (2 to 2⅜ in) tall, produces small to medium-sized, azure-blue flowers of peculiar brilliancy in September–October. Very floriferous. The flowers have a purple tinge on the exterior.

'Gloriosa' Raised by Eschmann in Switzerland. A vigorous variety with very large, broad flowers of bright delphinium-blue with a white throat. About 12cm (4¾ in) tall. Flowering time August–October.

'Goliath', raised by Eschmann from 'Macaulayi' × 'Inverleith'. Large flowers of pure Prussian-blue in September–October. Dark violet-brownish yellow stripes on the outside. About 12cm (4¾ in) tall.

'Hexa-farreri' A hybrid between *G. hexaphylla* × *G. farreri*. A good grower and often begins to flower in August. More compact than *G. farreri*, but grows more vigorously and has larger flowers than *G. hexaphylla*. The flowers have six corolla lobes with long points. There is also an 'Aberchalder' form with deep sky-blue flowers.

The cultivar 'Sensation' raised by Eschmann has deep azure-blue flowers striped with imperial purple on the exterior. Height 6 to 8cm (2⅜ to 3³⁄₁₆ in). Flowering time August–November.

'Ida K.' A *G. ornata* seedling from seed collected in Nepal. Not a hybrid but a local geographical form.

'Inez Weeks' A 'Hexa-farreri' seedling with considerably paler flowers, 10 to 14 in number on each stem. Very vigorous.

'Inshriach Hybrids' ('Kingfisher' × 'Kidbrooke Seedling') Raised by Jack Drake in Scotland. Late flowering from September to November, with deep-ultramarine flowers; 8cm (3³⁄₁₆ in) tall.

'Inverleith Seedling' Paler than 'Inverleith'. Raised by Jack Drake, the colour can be described as a brilliant budgerigar-blue. White throats; 8 to 10cm (3³⁄₁₆ to 4 in) tall.

'Inverleith' (*G. farreri* × *G. veitchiorum*) One of the older standard varieties with very large 10cm (4 in) deep-blue flowers in August–November. Outstandingly floriferous. Older plants tend to become rather leggy and less compact. Often somewhat susceptible to disease.

'Kidbrooke Seedling' The parents are sometimes stated as *G. farreri* × *G. ornata*, and sometimes as *G. sino ornata* × *G. farreri*. Similar to *G. sino ornata*, but flowers three weeks earlier. About 8cm (3³⁄16 in) tall, with brilliant French-blue flowers.

Also offered under the name 'Kidbrooke Seedling No. 6' (Drake) is a variety with deep Cambridge-blue flowers, their brilliance heightened by a white throat.

'Kidora' A seedling from 'Kidbrooke Seedling' × *G. ornata*.

'Kingfisher' Sold under this name is a form of × *macaulayi* which resembles *G. sino ornata* and flowers in August–September, but has larger flowers and darker leaves. Widely grown in Great Britain and easily propagated by division in spring. A variety which every gardener simply must have. Jack Drake's best × *macaulayi* selection.

'Kobaltauge' Raised from Eschmann in Switzerland from 'Kidbrooke Seedling' × *G. veitchiorum*. About 8cm (3³⁄16 in) tall, flowers of warm, brilliant ultramarine-blue with a purple sheen, from August to September.

'Kolibri' From Eschmann in Switzerland, only 5 to 8cm (2 to 3³⁄16 in) tall. Very small flowers of brilliant azure-blue with white throats in August–October.

'Lucerna' An 'Inverleith' seedling. One of the best varieties raised by Eschmann. A very good grower, about 12cm (4¾ in) tall, large flowered and with a long flowering season from August to November. Flowers brilliant sapphire-blue with white throats.

× macaulayi One of the oldest and most widely grown hybrids of this group. Raised from *G. sino ornata* × *G. farreri*. A good grower, somewhat similar to *G. sino ornata*, but the flowers are paler and the calyx lobes longer. Leaves darker in colour and slightly reflexed. Various selections have been made from this standard hybrid. Propagated by division.

× macaulayi 'Selektion Eschmann' Pure ultramarine-blue with a white interior, about 10cm (4 in) tall.

× macaulayi 'Wellsii' Somewhat lighter blue with striping on the exterior.

'Magnificent' (*G. veitchiorum* × *macaulayi*) Flowers somewhat larger and wider than those of *G. veitchiorum*, of brilliant, deep royal-blue, with stripes on the exterior. Six to 8cm (2⅜ to 3³⁄₁₆ in) tall, it flowers from August to November. Raised by Eschmann in Switzerland.

'Midnight' (*G. sino ornata* × *G. veitchiorum*) A pretty variety with deep-blue flowers devoid of stripes or spots. Eight to 10cm (3³⁄₁₆ to 4 in) tall, flowering time September to November.

'Mount Everest' A white-flowered strain from Holland. Ten to 12cm (4 to 4¾ in) tall, flowers August–October.

'Nibelungen' An 'Inverleith' seedling. A vigorous grower, large dark-blue flowers with a white throat. About 11cm (4⁵⁄₁₆ in) tall, long flowering season from August to November.

'Omega' Another seedling from the 'Hexa-farreri' complex raised by Jack Drake in Scotland. Eight to 10cm (3³⁄₁₆ to 4 in) tall, beautifully shaped flowers of brilliant dark-blue, striped internally. Vigorous and easily propagated.

'Opal' (× *G. veitchiorum*) Raised by Eschmann in Switzerland. Pure brilliant opal-blue flowers with a white throat, appearing in August to November. Height 8 to 10cm (3³⁄₁₆ to 4 in).

'Orphylla' (*G. ornata* × *G. hexaphylla*) A compact plant with pale-blue flowers with a white throat. The corolla has six lobes.

'Orva' (*G. ornata* × *G. veitchiorum*) Small, deep cobalt-blue flowers with dark-purple lines in the interior. A stocky plant, about 6 to 7cm (2⅜ to 2¾ in) tall, flowering in August to October.

'Pilatusgeist' Raised by Eschmann in Switzerland from 'Inverleith' × *G. veitchiorum*. Brilliant delphinium-blue flowers with white throats and clear stripes on the exterior. Flowers August–October, height 10 to 12cm (4 to 4¾ in).

'Reuss' Raised by Eschmann, Switzerland. Shining butterfly-blue with a white throat and fine dots in the interior. About 12cm (4¾ in) tall, flowers August–September.

'Saphir' (× *G. veitchiorum*) Raised by Eschmann, Switzerland. Dark sapphire-blue with a white throat. Flowers September–November, 10 to 12cm (4 to 4¾ in) tall.

'Sensation' A novelty raised by Eschmann in Switzerland. Deep azure-blue; imperial purple externally with pronounced stripes. Six to 8cm (2⅜ to 3³⁄₁₆ in) tall, flowers August–November.

'Sinora' (*G. sino ornata* × *G. ornata*) Deep butterfly-blue flowers with a narrow corolla.

'Splendeur' Raised by Eschmann in Switzerland. Butterfly-blue with a white throat, the edges of the corolla lobes tinged with red. Broad, dumpy flowers. Flowering time August–October. Height 9cm (3½ in).

'Starlight' (× *G. veitchiorum*) Raised by Eschmann in Switzerland. A small-growing variety, 7 to 8cm (2¾ to 3³⁄₁₆ in) high, with brilliant azure-blue flowers in August–October.

× **Stevenagensis** (*G. sino ornata* × *G. veitchiorum*) Differs from *G. sino ornata* in having stems with more branches, a narrower corolla tube and a deeper colour. Flowers deep purple with greenish-yellow lines and spots inside. Flowers August–November, 8 to 10cm (3³⁄₁₆ to 4 in) tall. Raised by F. Barker at Stevenage. There is also a selected form sold under the name 'Frank Barker'.

'Susan Jane' A seedling from 'Inverleith' raised by Jack Drake in Scotland. Intense azure-blue with a white throat. Corolla lobes deeply notched. A good grower with creeping stems. Early flowering, August–November. Height 6 to 8cm (2⅜ to 3³⁄₁₆ in).

'Thunersee' ('Inverleith' × *G. veitchiorum*) Raised by Eschmann in Switzerland. A splendid sapphire-blue, somewhat paler than 'Inverleith', with a white throat. Intermediate between 'Kingfisher' and *G. sino ornata*. Flowers August–October. Vigorous, about 10cm (4 in) tall.

'Veora' (*G. veitchiorum* × *G. ornata*) Raised by G. H. Berry. Glossy, fresh-green leaves, long flower stalks and brilliant azure-blue flowers with white throats. A long flowering season from August to October; 8 to 10cm (3³⁄₁₆ to 4 in) tall.

'VIP' (*G. veitchiorum* × 'Inverleith parents') Dark ultramarine-blue with a purple sheen, 6 to 7cm (2⅜ to 2¾ in) tall, August –November.

'Vorna' (like 'Veora', from *G. veitchiorum* × *G. ornata*) Raised by Dr W. L. Lead, Stockport. In colour, this hybrid comes very close to the spring-flowering trumpet gentian; the hue might be described as deep 'Prussian blue'. Long vigorous shoots from a central rosette. About 12cm (4¾ in) tall, flowers September–November.

'Wealdensis' (*G.* × 'Hexa-farreri' × *G. veitchiorum*) Healthy growth with large, deep-blue flowers, 10cm (4 in) tall. Corolla lobes deeply reflexed.

'Wellensittich' (budgerigar) Raised by Eschmann in Switzerland. Large, elegantly shaped flowers, pure butterfly-blue with a white throat. About 12cm (4¾ in) tall, flowers August–November.

'Zauberglocke' ('Inverleith' × *G. veitchiorum*) Raised by Eschmann in Switzerland. The earliest dark-purple variety, flowering July-October, about 8cm (3¾ in) tall.

'Zauberland' From 'Inverleith'. Larger flowers than its parent, French blue. Flowering time August–October, about 12cm (4¾ in) tall. Not very strong growing, but eagerly sought after by enthusiasts.

Acaulis forms and hybrids Any description of gentian hybrids must include the *acaulis* complex. Many of the garden forms of the 'trumpet gentian' have been in cultivation for so long that their origins are no longer ascertainable. Indeed, it is often impossible to say whether they are hybrids between species of Section Thylactitis (Megalanthe) or outstandingly vigorous local geographical forms of one of the species. In the list which follows no attempt has been made to draw this distinction.

'Angustifolia-Hybrids Frei' A magnificent, highly floriferous variety with large flowers, raised by Messrs Frei, Wildensbuch, Switzerland. In the author's garden—on soil containing lime—this has proved one of the best varieties. Should be divided and replanted as soon as flowering starts to slacken.

'Coelestina' Probably the palest-coloured variety of the *acaulis* group. Large, funnel-shaped flowers of pure sky-blue with deeply indented, pointed corolla lobes. Flowering season April–May, often with a further flush in October–November, about 12cm (4¾ in) tall.

'Dinarica' This is not the species *G. dinarica* from the wild, but a selection made by Messrs Härlen. A free-flowering commercial variety, with clear ultramarine-blue flowers. Taller than the species, with long flower stalks. About 12cm (4¾ in) tall when the seeds are ripe. Flowering time April–May, with a further flush in October–November.

'Gedanensis' Raised by Wocke in Danzig (Gedania = Danzig). A garden variety, 12cm (4¾ in) tall, with large flowers. The pure, ultramarine-blue, bell-shaped flowers are 4 to 4.5cm (about 1¾ in) in diameter, with very short stalks and spreading calyx teeth. Flowering time April–May, with a further flush in October–November.

'Holzmann' Also known as *G. holzmannii*. A long-stalked *G. angustifolia* hybrid with large, deep azure-blue flowers 4.5 to 5cm (about 1¾ in) in diameter with olive-green spots in the tube. Corolla lobes deeply notched. Flowers in April–May, with a further flush in autumn.

'Krumrey-Enzian' In the 1960s and afterwards a gentian of the *acaulis* group attracted notice by its profusion of brilliant-blue flowers. It was sold under the name 'Krumrey-Enzian', having originated in the Bavarian nursery of that name from a cross between a blue type with a slight reddish tinge from the Carpathians and an alpine form of the *acaulis* group. The botanical identity of the parent species or subspecies is unknown.

'Maxima' A beautiful variety with dark azure-blue flowers with a reddish sheen, 10cm (4 in) tall, and with wide corolla tubes. Noted for its autumn flowering.

'Nymphenburgensis' Though highly praised by Karl Foerster it is doubtful whether this form is still in existence. Noted for its profusion of flowering when grown on loamy soils.

'Saturn' Raised by Eschmann in Switzerland. A later-flowering hybrid with large, pale-blue flowers with a short, broad calyx and corolla lobes. Flowering time May–June, height about 12cm (4¾ in).

'Undulatifolia' Not to be confused with *G. clusii* var. *undulatifolia*; this variety was raised by Jack Drake in Scotland. About 12cm (4¾ in) tall, with bright ultramarine flowers.

Gentiana × *suendermannii*

A rather mysterious plant, its origins still obscure despite numerous enquiries. It flowers at the end of August or beginning of September, somewhat later than *G. septemfida* var. *lagodechiana*, which it resembles in habit though it has shorter, broader stem leaves and a stiffer, more upright mode of growth, not prostrate or sprawling. Height 12 to 20cm (4¾ to 8 in) with a less racemose inflorescence, sometimes even single flowered. Grown in a place where it is happy, it sometimes produces flowers with as many as eight to ten corolla lobes. It requires stony soil in a sunny position and is a lime-hater; in soil of neutral reaction it will survive but does not flourish.

Certain hybrids have been produced in Japan from a totally different range of parent species. They are:

Gentiana × *brevidens* Fr. et Sav. (*G. makinoi* × *G. scabra* var. *buergeri*) and *G.* × *iseana* Makino (*G. scabra* var. *buergeri* × *G. sikokiana*). Neither of them has yet appeared in Europe. Two further gentian hybrids are marketed on a commercial scale in Japan. The first originated from a cross between *G. triflora* Pall. var. *japonica* Hara × *G. makinoi*. It furnishes cut flowers in late summer for vases and flower arranging (Ikebana). It may have some connection with *G.* 'Royal Blue' now in cultivation in Europe. The second is known as *G.* 'Hybrida hort.' and is very popular as a pot plant in the autumn. It is raised on a large scale from cuttings taken in June and grown in plastic pots. Mass production has made these pot gentians comparatively inexpensive (1 or 2 US $ per pot). Besides the blue form there are also pink and white forms.

In Great Britain there is a hybrid known under the name *G.* × *hascombensis*; as already mentioned in the section on *G. septemfida*, it is a hybrid between two forms or varieties of that species.

Also recorded in Great Britain is a hybrid with the name *G.* 'Birch Hybrid' (*G. pneumonanthe* × *G. septemfida* var. *lagodechiana*). It has stout, erect stems, 30cm (12 in) tall, in habits resembling *G. pneumonanthe*, carrying several tubular flowers, widely open at the mouth, in a delicate shade of blue, the interiors richly sprinkled with white.

Gentiana ishizuchii

In recent years this gorgeous rose-pink gentian has spread from Japan. Contrary to what might be thought from its botanical-sounding name, it is not a true species but an attractive colour variant of a hybrid gentian grown on a commercial scale in Japan and named after Mount Ishizuchi (Shikoku). This gentian is cultivated in and distributed by Japanese nurseries which raise alpine plants. According to Japanese records it is thought to be a hybrid between *G.* Bunge var. *buergeri* f. *procumbens* Toyokumi and *G. septemfida*. It has dark-rose, pink or red flowers and is 20cm (8 in) tall, somewhat resembling *G. septemfida* in habit. The best mode of propagation is by cuttings in June. A fairly acid compost is essential for successful cultivation.

Certain older publications contain various interesting hybrid names, some of them coined by combining the names of their parents, though nowadays they are no longer current. For example, *Möller's Deutsche Gartner-Zeitung* in 1903 listed the following hybrids:

G. angubavarica Gusm. = *G. angulosa* × *G. bavarica*

G. angubrachyphylla Gusm. = *G. angulosa* × *G. brachyphylla*

G. vernabrachya Gusm. = *G. verna* × *G. brachyphylla*

G. bavarabrachya Gusm. = *G. bavarica* × *G. brachyphylla*

G. pumilimbricata Gusm. = *G. pumila* × *G. imbricata*

G. vernapula Gusm. = *G. verna* × *G. pumila*

G. burserlutea Gusm. = *G. burseri* × *G. lutea*

G. charpentieri Thom. = *G. lutea* × *G. punctata*

G. gaudiniana Thom. (*G. spuria* Leb.) = *G. punctata* × *G. purpurea*

G. kummeriana Sendt. (*G. haengsti* Hausm.) = *G. lutea* × *G. pannonica*

G. pannopurpurea Gusm. = *G. pannonica* × *G. purpurea*

G. thomasii Hall. fil (*G. rubra* Clairv.) = *G. purpurea* × *G. lutea*

Future prospects

What can be expected from the raising of new hybrid gentians? Among the Asiatic autumn-flowering gentians (Section Frigidae) vigour of growth, flower size and flower colour have now reached a level where there is little room for further advance. What we need are plants more tolerant of lime. *G. farreri* and some of its hybrids will accept a certain amount of lime though they do not really like it. Most of the other species, notably *G. sino ornata*, are poisoned by the least trace of lime.

Great advances have also been made in raising hybrids from the *acaulis* group. However, commercial growers would certainly like flowers with longer stems for little bouquets and other uses in the florist's shop.

There are as yet undreamt-of possibilities among the North American and Asiatic species. Such crossings might well result in plants which would produce splendid cut-flowers for commercial purposes. However, breeders should remember the difficulties encountered in growing *G.* 'Royal Blue' and should strive to raise plants which are lime tolerant.

Gentianella anglica (Pugsley) E. F. Warburg

Occurs in England on calcareous meadows. A biennial species up to 20cm (8 in) tall. Dull-purple flowers on stems which are usually little branched.

Gentianella anisodonta (Borbás) A. et D. Löve

Alps, Apennines, north-western Yogoslavia, on limestone soils. Closely similar to *G. pilosa*, but the lower stem leaves are obovate to spatulate and the upper leaves triangular-lanceolate; two of the corolla lobes are broader than the others. Corolla 2 to 3cm (¾ to 1¹⁄₁₆ in), reddish purple.

Gentianella aspera (Hegetschw. et Heer) Sotal.

Eastern and central Alps, uplands of southern Germany and western Czechoslovakia. A biennial up to 40cm (16 in) tall, usually branching from the base. The stem leaves are oval to oval-lanceolate or oval-triangular. The corolla is 1 to 4cm (⅜ to 1⅝ in) in diameter, violet, pink or whitish.

Gentianella aurea (L.), Harry Smith

Arctic coastal and riverside districts. An annual or biennial up to 50cm (20 in) tall with long, erect stems branching from the base. Stem leaves two or three times longer than broad. Small flowers, divided into four or five parts at the ends of the stems, usually surrounded by the upper stem leaves. Corolla 0.7 to 1cm (under ⅜ in) long, pale yellow, rarely blue.

Gentianella austriaca (A. et J. Kerner) J. Holub.

Eastern and central Europe. A biennial, usually 10 to 20cm (4 to 8 in) tall, branching from the base. Stem leaves oval-lanceolate to lanceolate. Flowers in corymbs, corolla 2.4 to 4.5cm (1 to 1¾ in) purplish-violet or whitish.

Gentianella barbata (Froel.) Berchtold et J. Presl

Northern and central Asia, Alaska, Canadian Yukon. Resembles *Gentianopsis detonsa* but is taller at 40cm (16 in). (In the writer's opinion this species should be assigned to the genus *Gentianopsis*.)

Gentianella barbellata Engelm.

A short-lived perennial which grows in thin woodland in Arizona,

Colorado and New Mexico. Five to 15cm (2 to 6 in) tall, with blue flowers in August–September.

Gentianella bulgarica (Velen.) J. Holub

Balkans. Long slender stems 5 to 20cm (2 to 8 in) tall, erect or sprawling, branching from the base. Stem leaves oblong-lanceolate. Flowers 1.2 to 2cm (½ to ¾ in) long, whitish or pale violet.

Gentianella campestris (L.) Börner (field gentian)

Pyrenees, Alps, Macedonia, Northern Apennines, Iceland, Great Britain and Ireland, on thin grassland, usually on limestone, seldom on igneous rock. An upright plant, 3 to 30cm (1³⁄₁₆ to 12 in) tall. Stems usually branched, often with a reddish tinge, leaves lanceolate. Calyx with four lobes, two large and two small. Corolla dull violet, rarely whitish, with a fringe of hairs in the throat. Flowers from June to September. Several subspecies.

Gentianella columnae (Ten.) J. Holub

Apennines. A biennial up to 15cm (6 in) tall, branching from the base. Stem leaves lanceolate, 1 to 2cm (⅜ to ¾ in) long, flowers purplish-violet or whitish.

Gentianella crispata (Vis.) J. Holub

Southern Italy, Balkans, in mountainous districts. A biennial, 2 to 20cm (¾ to 8 in) tall, the base usually covered with dried remnants of last year's foliage. Basal leaves obovate to spatulate, stem leaves more lanceolate. Flowers in a corymb, violet or whitish, 1.5 to 2cm (½ to ¾ in) long. Calyx lobes crinkled with a blackish margin.

Gentianella diemensis (Griseb.) J. H. Willis

Mountains of southern Australia and Tasmania. Forms loose clumps 10 to 25 or occasionally 30cm (up to 12 in) tall. Basal leaves opposite. Flowers in five parts, white or cream-coloured with fine blue or violet veins, solitary or in a lax corymb. Flowers in February–March in its native country; very pretty.

Gentianella engadinensis (Wettst.) J. Holub

Alps. Closely similar to *G. pilosa*, but has oval-lanceolate stem leaves and unequal calyx lobes.

Related genera

Gentianella

The genus *Gentianella* Moench consists of annuals or biennials usually having stems which begin to branch just above the basal rosette. The calyx is divided to at least half way and has four or five lobes not joined by an inner membrane. The corolla is cylindrical or obconical with four or five more or less patent lobes, without a small lobe in the sinus. The corolla is usually fringed or ciliate in the throat.

In general the plants resemble those of the genus *Gentiana*, the main difference being the absence of minor lobes or scales between the corolla lobes and the presence of fringes in the throat.

Thc genus *Gentianella* is of little or no garden value, yet it contains some pretty species often encountered in the wild. Seeds are offered in the seed lists produced by amateur societies and have even begun to appear in the catalogues of certain seed merchants. Consequently, the genus should not be entirely ignored, especially as many of its species were once included in older writings under the name *Gentiana*.

Botanists subdivide the genus *Gentianella* into Sections Comastoma, Gentianella and Arctophila. These are solely of botanical importance, and the species are listed here in alphabetical order.

To establish them in the rock garden or other suitable places is not always easy. Early sowings in boxes, cold frames or at the spot where they are to flower seem to offer the best prospects of success. Seedlings should not be allowed to grow too large before being pricked out or planted out.

Gentianella amarella (L.). Börner, Felwort

Northern and central Europe, the Ukraine, northern North America. An annual or biennial plant 15 to 50cm (6 to 20 in) tall. The upper leaves are lanceolate and subacute, the lower leaves spatulate or ovate with blunt points. The flowers vary from purple-violet and blue to greenish-yellow or white; they are 1 to 2cm (3/8 to 3/4 in) long and are carried in clusters in the upper leaf axils.

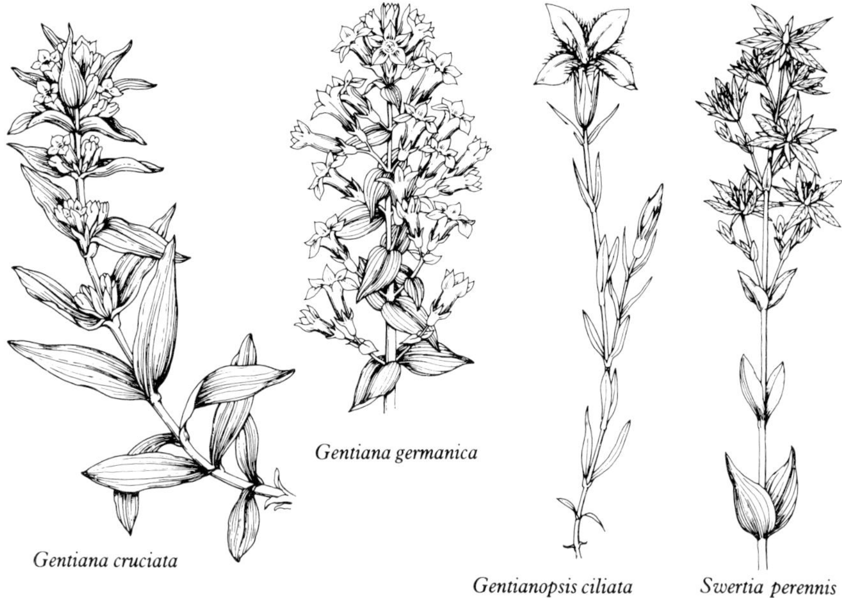

Figure 16 Familiar plants from some of the genera of the gentian family

Gentianella falcata (Turcz. ex Karchin et Kir.) Harry Smith

Pakistan and south-western China, usually on dry soils in open situations. All the leaves are basal and elliptic, about 1cm ($\frac{3}{8}$ in) long. Numerous erect stems 6 to 10cm ($2\frac{3}{8}$ to 4 in) tall, ending in solitary flowers. Flowers deep blue/violet with white hairs in the throat, 1 to 2cm ($\frac{3}{8}$ to $\frac{3}{4}$ in) long, with five, oval, spreading corolla lobes. Flowers August–September.

Gentianella formosissima (Don) Gilg.

A handsome South American species more than 1m (3 ft) tall. Stems abundantly branched with long, broad, lanceolate leaves. Flowers very numerous, 3 to 5cm ($1\frac{3}{16}$ to 2 in) long, purple or dark pink, on long stalks.

Gentianella germanica (Willd.) E. F. Warburg (German gentian)

Central Europe, from Sweden to the Carpathians, on thin pastures, mainly on damp, calcareous soil. An erect, often little-branched plant 5 to 35 cm (2 in to 2ft 2 in) tall. The basal leaf rosette has usually withered by flowering time. Flowers reddish-violet, rarely white, funnel shaped. Corolla lobes up to 15mm (5⁄8 in) long, with hairs in the throat. Flowers from May to October.

Gentianella hypericifolia (Murb.) Pritchard

Western and central Pyrenees. Closely resembles *G. campestris*, but stem leaves are elliptic to broad ovate, and calyx lobes are widest at the middle. Corolla 2.5cm (1 in), often whitish.

Gentianella lutescens (Velen.) J. Holub

Eastern and central Europe and northern Balkans, mainly in mountainous districts. A biennial up to 40cm (16 in) tall, simple or branching, with a racemose inflorescence. Stem leaves narrow oval. Corolla 1.8 to 2.5cm (3⁄4 to 1 in), purple or yellowish.

Gentianella moorcroftiana (Wallich ex G. Don) Airy Shaw

Pakistan to central Nepal in open situations and places kept moist by trickling water. An annual, usually much branched plant 5 to 20cm (2 to 8 in) tall with lanceolate leaves 1.5 to 3cm (5⁄8 to 13⁄16 in) long. The basal leaves have usually disappeared at flowering time. Numerous pale-blue to dark-mauve, funnel-shaped flowers in loose clusters. Corolla 1.5cm (5⁄8 in) long when flowering begins, lengthening at maturity. Flowering time August–October.

Gentianella nana (Wulfen) Pritchard

Eastern Alps, on limestone, in moist screes and snow patch hollows. Closely resembles *G. tenella*, but only 2 to 3cm (3⁄4 to 13⁄16 in) tall, and the flower stalks are not more than twice as long as the flowers. Flowers dark blue.

Gentianella padulosa (Hook.) Harry Smith

Pakistan to south-western China in open situations and among dwarf shrubs. A slender annual up to 30cm (12 in) tall with long-stalked, solitary, blue or white flowers, erect or drooping. The leaves are narrow elliptic, blunt pointed and 2 to 4cm (3⁄4 to 15⁄8 in) long. The corolla tube is up to 3.5cm (13⁄8 in) long and has four rounded or broad elliptic, blue, spreading lobes. No hairs or fringes in the throat. Flowering time July–August.

Gentianella pedunculata (D. Don) Harry Smith

Pakistan to south-eastern Tibet in open situations. Closely resembles *G. falcata*, but the latter species is distinguished by the unequal calyx lobes and by the length of the calyx, which is less than one-third of the length of the corolla tube. Flowering time August–October.

Gentianella propinqua (Richardson) J. M. Gillet

From Alaska and the Yukon to British Columbia and Montreal and Quebec. An annual plant up to 35cm (14 in) tall, forming rosettes of elliptic to spatulate leaves about 3.5cm ($1\frac{3}{8}$ in) long. Stem leaves narrower. Flowers pale violet to violet, solitary or in small clusters, terminal and axillary, 2cm ($\frac{3}{4}$ in) long, funnel shaped.

Gentianella pygmaea Regel et Schmalh.

Central Asia, Pamirs, on mountain sedge meadows, 4,000 to 4,200m (13,100 to 13,800 ft), very rare. An annual plant with narrow rosettes of lanceolate leaves 2 to 6mm ($\frac{1}{16}$ to $\frac{1}{4}$ in) long. Total height 1 to 4cm ($\frac{3}{8}$ to $1\frac{5}{8}$ in). Flowers 7 to 8mm ($\frac{1}{4}$ to $\frac{5}{16}$ in) long, cream coloured. Flowering time July–August.

Gentianella quinquefolia (L.) Small

Eastern North America. An annual or sometimes biennial plant 30 to 60cm (12 to 24 in) tall, branching above. Leaves oval, pointed. Flowers pale lilac to deep blue, 2.5cm (1 in) long, in terminal clusters of three to five.

Gentianella ramosa (Hegetschw.) J. Holub

Central and south-western Alps, on limestone soils. A biennial up to 15cm (6 in) tall, normally branching from the base and hence having a bushy appearance. Stem leaves oval-lanceolate to lanceolate. Corolla 1 to 2cm ($\frac{3}{8}$ to $\frac{3}{4}$ in), pale violet or whitish.

Gentianella tenella (Rootb.) Börner

Widely distributed: Spain, Pyrenees, Alps, Carpathians, eastwards to central asia, North America. On limestone and igneous rocks, in short grass and screes. Up to 10cm (4 in) tall, stems branching at the base, with one to two leaves. Flowers lilac, pale violet, rarely white. Corolla lobes four, not spreading. Flowers July–September.

Gentianella turkestanorum Holub

Central Asia, Pamirs, on mountain meadows, rarely in groups, but everywhere frequent at altitudes from 1,700 to 3,600m (5,500 to 11,800 ft). A biennial 3 to 20cm (1 3/16 to 8 in) tall with two to four pink flowers 9 to 19mm (1/4 to 3/4 in) long. Rosette leaves narrow linear, 10 to 35mm (3/8 to 1 3/8 in) long; stalks always clearly recognisable. Flowering time May–July. Seed is occasionally offered.

Gentianella weberbaueri Gilg.

A South American species found in rocks and scree at high altitudes. The tight rosette puts up a single stem 30 to 50cm (12 to 20 in) tall with red flowers at the apex.

Gentianella yabei Hara

Japan, a rare biennial 5 to 40cm (2 to 16 in) tall, erect, unbranched or little branched, with pale-blue flowers 2.5 to 3.5cm (1 to 1 3/8 in) long.

Gentianopsis (fringed gentian)

In certain publications (including *Flora Europaea*) the species of the newly founded genus *Gentianopsis* Ma are still included under *Gentiana* and *Gentianella*. However, its standing as a separate genus can hardly be disputed. The genus comprises some 15 species or a few more, all annuals or biennials and none of much garden value. However, seed is offered in the seed exchanges and the most important species will therefore be briefly described. The flowers are divided into four parts and the corolla lobes are fringed.

Gentianopsis ciliata (L.) Ma (fringed gentian)

Central and southern Europe, the Caucasus, Near East. On thin grassland and dry meadows, at forest margins, seldom above 2,000m (6,500 ft). Usually on soil rich in minerals, especially on limestone, seldom in marshy spots. Late flowering, August–November. A biennial or perennial species, 7 to 25cm (2 3/4 to 10 in) tall, with erect, ascending stems, sometimes branched, with opposite linear-lanceolate leaflets. These stems carry a single, terminal, cornflower-blue flower divided into four parts. The flower is funnel shaped to bell shaped and has four ovate spreading lobes, with conspicuous fringes at their margins.

Though of common occurrence it is certainly not a garden plant, being very difficult in cultivation. However, it is always a delight to encounter it on autumn rambles in the mountains. Seed is offered from time to time, and direct sowing in the rock garden at the spot where it is to flower offers the best prospect of success.

Gentianopsis contorta (Royle) Ma

Himalaya, Japan, Manchuria and China. An erect, biennial species, 5 to 10cm (2 to 4 in) tall, unbranched or little branched. Corolla tubular, pale mauve.

Gentianopsis crinita (Froel.) Ma

Eastern North America. An annual plant up to 90cm (3 ft) tall with deep-blue flowers, occasionally white, growing singly or in small groups. Flowers up to 5cm (2 in) long, corolla lobes fringed. Leaves oval to lanceolate.

Gentianopsis detonsa (Rottb.) Ma

Arctic and subarctic Europe in wet places near the coast. An annual or biennial plant 5 to 25cm (2 to 10 in) tall with spatulate basal leaves and two or three pairs of linear-lanceolate stem leaves. Flowers dark blue, 3.5 to 4cm (1⅜ to 1⅝ in) long, often with a few short fringes at the margins.

The species *G. halopetala* and *G. thermalis*, though described separately below, are assigned to this species by some botanists.

Gentianopsis halopetala (A. Gray) Iltis (sierra gentian)

Californian mountains. An erect annual or biennial, 30cm (12 in) tall or more. Leaves mostly near the base, obovate to linear, up to 3.8cm (1½ in) long. Flowers solitary, 3.5 to 5cm (1⅜ to 2 in) long, rich blue.

Gentianopsis procera (T. Holm) Ma

North America, in wet places. Similar to *G. crinita*, but has linear-lanceolate leaves, and the corolla lobes are fringed along the sides only.

Gentianopsis stricta Ikonn.

Pamir mountains. Frequent in meadows from 1,800 to 4,000m (5,900 to 13,100 ft). An annual 5 to 25cm (2 to 10 in) tall with brilliant-blue flowers.

Gentianopsis thermalis (O. Kuntze) Iltis (fringed Rocky Mountain gentian)

Colorado, Arizona. Grows near the hot springs in Yellowstone National Park (hence the name). A slender annual up to 30cm (12 in) tall. Leaves obovate, flowers up to 5cm (2 in) long, deep blue, often with pale-blue stripes.

Megacodon

Megacodon stylophora (C. B. Clarke) Harry Smith

Nepal, south-eastern Tibet and western China at 4,000m (13,100 ft) and higher. A robust plant up to 1.8 m (6 ft) or taller. Basal leaves elliptic, about 30cm (12 in) long, stem leaves 15cm (6 in). Flowers short stalked, terminal and axillary. Calyx broad tubular, about 1.8cm (¾ in) long, calyx lobes oval. Corolla broad tubular, 6.5cm (2½ in) long, pale yellow. Flowers in July–August. The Asiatic counterpart of *Gentiana lutea*.

An unmistakable plant, distinguishable from *Gentiana lutea* by its broad, tubular flowers. It requires deep soil in an open position. Seldom seen in gardens.

Swertia

The species of the genus *Swertia* L., though not widely grown, are of interest to the experienced plantsman. While not as attractive as the true gentians, they have a quiet natural beauty which appeals to the connoisseur. Some require wet boggy conditions (peat bed), others like acid woodland soil rich in humus, but there are a few which are content with ordinary garden soil. Hot summers are fatal to many species of *Swertia*, and a cool place should therefore be chosen. Most species are propagated by seed, but older plants can sometimes be divided.

Swertia occurs in Europe and in the temperate zones of Asia, North America and Africa, though concentrated in eastern Asia. Some 50 or more species are known, though the taxonomy is confused. Some botanists recognise the genus *Frasera*, but others include it in *Swertia*.

Swertia includes both annual and perennial species. The leaves are usually opposite and entire, the flowers usually blue, more rarely white, in panicles. The parts of the flower are in fives, or sometimes in fours.

The corolla is circular, each corolla lobe having a pair of nectaries at the base. The styles are short or absent.

Plants are not easily available. A few species may be found in specialist alpine nurseries, but otherwise the only source of supply is seed, occasionally to be found in the seed-exchange lists.

Swertia alternifolia Royle

Himalaya. A perennial, easily recognisable by its flowers, few in number but large, pale yellow with blue stamens. Flowers up to 2.5cm (1 in) in diameter. Plants 15 to 25cm (6 to 10 in) tall with slender stems. Basal leaves up to 10cm (4 in) long. Most attractive.

Swertia aucheri Boiss.

Armenia, Iran. A perennial with oblong leaves narrowing towards the points. Flowers yellowish.

Swertia bimaculata Hook. f. et T. Thoms.

Eastern Himalaya. A much branched annual plant sometimes growing as tall as a man. Leaves elliptic, up to 15cm (6 in) long, three veined, tapering to the stalk. Many flowered inflorescence. Flowers whitish or yellowish-green, with black spots in the upper half.

Swertia cuneata D. Don

Himalaya, on alpine hillsides. An erect perennial 10 to 25cm (4 to 10 in) tall with spatulate leaves 3.5 to 7.5cm (1⅜ to 3 in) long, the lower leaves stalked and the upper leaves almost sessile. Leaf stalks winged. Flowers 2.5 to 3.5cm (1 to 1⅜ in) in diameter, long stalked, dusky blue. Flowering time August–October.

Swertia fedtschenkoana Pissjauk.

Pamirs, on wet mountain meadows, rather rare. A perennial 40 to 50cm (16 to 20 in) tall with broad, lanceolate leaves and greenish flowers in July.

Swertia hookeri C. B. Clarke

Eastern Nepal to south-eastern Tibet, on open hillsides. A robust, erect plant. Flowers in dense, short-stalked whorls, bell shaped with spreading corolla lobes, maroon coloured with dark nerves. Inflorescence terminal, forming an interrupted spike. Basal leaves 15 to 20cm (6 to 8 in) long, spatulate-elliptic, upper stem leaves tinged with purple. Flowering time June–September.

Swertia juzepczukii Pissjauk.

Pamirs, mountain meadows, rather uncommon. A perennial 30 to 50cm (12 to 20 in) tall with greenish flowers in June–July.

Swertia marginata Schrenk

Pamirs, frequently found on mountain meadows. Five to 20cm (2 to 8 in) tall with greenish flowers in July.

Swertia multicaulis D. Don

Himalaya. A perennial about 20cm (8 in) tall. Leaves narrow oblong to spatulate, about 5cm (2 in) long. Unlike other species, its stems are much branched from the base. Flowers long stalked, slate blue, in a much branched inflorescence. Corolla lobes 0.8 to 1.3cm (5⁄16 to ½ in) long, blunt. Recommended as a pretty plant for the rock garden. Flowering time June–September.

Swertia perennis L.

Europe, Asia, North America (from California to Alaska) in calcareous fens and bogs up to 1,800m (5,900 ft). Perennial, 15 to 40cm (6 to 16 in) tall, usually about 30cm (12 in), with opposite, ovate to elliptic, bluish-green stem leaves. The basal leaves are oblong-elliptic and long-stalked. The erect angular stem is seldom branched. The terminal, steel-blue flowers are star shaped, with five parts. There are also darker and almost white forms, sometimes spotted greenish or white. An enthusiast's plant for boggy, peaty places.

Japanese alpine nurseries offer *S. perennis* var. *cuspidata*, which grows only 10 to 20cm (4 to 8 in) tall. Another variety is *S. perennis* var. *stenopetala* (Regel et Tiling) Maxim., with smaller flowers (Japan, Sakhalin, Kurile Islands, Siberia, Alaska).

Swertia perfoliata Royle ex G. Don

SYNONYM: *S. speciosa* Wallich ex D. Don (not G. Don)

A perennial up to 1m (3 ft) tall, stems hollow, leaves opposite, seven veined. Basal leaves long stalked, elliptic-lanceolate, up to 20cm (8 in) long. Stem leaves up to 12cm (4¾ in) long, joined at their bases into a sheath about 1.2cm (½ in) long. The inflorescence is a narrow panicle. Corolla white with irregular blue spots.

Swertia petiolata Royle ex D. Don

Himalaya. Resembles *S. perfoliata*. Distinguished mainly by its five-veined leaves and its seeds. Flowering time July–August.

Swertia schugnanica Pissjauk.

SYNONYM: *S. lactea*

Pamir, on short sedge-turf, mountain meadows, usually singly, rarely in groups. A perennial about 60cm (24 in) tall with greenish-white flowers in June–July.

Summaries and Lists

Synonyms of gentian species

Chondrophylla fremontii = *Gentiana aquatica L.*
Dasystephana affinis (Griseb.) Rydb. = *Gentiana affinis* Griseb.
– *andrewsii* (Griseb.) Small = *Gentiana andrewsii* Griseb.
– *calycosa* Rydb. = *Gentiana calycosa* Griseb.
– *flavida* (Gray) Britt. = *Gentiana andrewsii* Griseb. f. *albiflora* Britt.
– *linearis* Britt. = *Gentiana linearis* Froel.
– *parryi* Rydb. = *Gentiana parryi* Engelm.
– *puberula* (Michx.) Small = *Gentiana puberulenta* Pringle
Ericoila clusii (Perr. et Song.) A. et D. Löve = *Gentiana clusii* Perr. et Song.
– *kochiana* (Perr. et Song.) A. et D. Löve = *Gentiana acaulis* L. s. str.
Gentiana acaulis L. p. p. = *Gentiana clusii* Perr. et Song.
– *alpina* L. var. *alpina* (Vill.) Griseb. = *Gentiana alpina* Vill.
– *algida* var. *igarashii* Miyabe et Kudo = *Gentiana algida* f. *igarashii* (Miyabe et Kudo) Toyokumi
– – var. *sibirica* Kusn. = *Gentiana algida* Pall.
– *amarella* L. = *Gentiana amarella* (L.) Börner
– *angulosa* Bieb. = *Gentiana verna* L.
– *anisodonta* Borbás. = *Gentianealla anisodonta* (Borbás) A. et D. Löve
– *aspera* Hegetschw. et Heer = *Gentianella aspera* (Hegetschw. et Heer) Dostál ex Skalický
– *aurea* L. = *Gentianella aurea* (L.) H. Sm.
– *austriaca* A. et J. Kerner = *Gentianella austriaca* (A. et J. Kerner) J. Holub
– *axillariflora* Lév. et Van = *Gentiana triflora* var. *japonica* (Kusn.) Hara
– – var. *horomuiensis* (Kudo) Hara = *Gentiana triflora* var. *horomuiensis* (Kudo) Hara
– *axillariflora* var. *montana* Hara = *Gentiana triflora* var. *montana* (Hara) Hara
– – var. *naitoana* Lév. et Faurie = *Gentiana triflora* var. *japonica* Kusn.) Hara
– *barbata* Froel. = *Gentianella barbata* (Froel.) Bercht. et J. Presl
– *Bigelovii* A. Gray = *Gentiana affinis* Griseb. ex Hook.

– *buergeri* Miq. = *Gentiana scabra* var. *buergeri* (Miq.) Maxim.
– *bulgarica* Velen. = *Gentianella bulgarica* (Velen.) J. Holub
– *caespitosa* Hayata = *Gentiana arisanensis* Hayata
– *calycina* (Koch) Wettst. = *Gentianella anisodonta* (Borbás) A. et D. Löve
– *campestris* L. = *Gentianella campestris* (L.) Börner
– *ciliata* L. = *Gentianopsis ciliata* (L.) Ma
– *columnae* Ten. = *Gentianella columnae* (Ten.) J. Holub
– *cordifolia* C. Koch = *Gentiana septemfida* Pall.
– *crinita* Froel. = *Gentianopsis crinita* (Froel.) Ma
– *crispata* Vis. = *Gentianella crispata* (Vis.) J. Holub
– *depressa* D. Don = *Gentiana stipitata* Edgew.
– *detonsa* Rottb. = *Gentianopsis detonsa* (Rottb.) Ma
– *elegans* A. Nels. = *Gentianopsis thermalis* (O. Kuntze) Iltis
– *elliotii* (Hapm. not Raf.) = *Gentiana catesbaei* Walt.
– *engadinensis* (Wettst.) Br.-Bl. et Samuelsson = *Gentianella engadinensis* (Wettst.) J. Holub
– *excisa* W. D. J. Koch = *Gentiana acaulis* L. s. str.
– *favratii* (Rittener) Favrat = *Gentiana brachyphylla* Vill. ssp. *favratii* (Rittener) Tutin
– *flavida* A. Gray = *Gentiana alba* Mühlenb.
– *fremontii* (Torr.) A. Nels. = *Gentiana aquatica* L.
– *frigida var. algida* (Pall.) Froel. = *Gentiana algida* Pall.
– *germanica* Willd. = *Gentianella germanica* (Willd.) E. F. Warburg
– – ssp. *bulgarica* (Velen.) Hayek = *Gentianella bulgarica* (Velen.) J. Holub
– – ssp. *calycina* (Koch) Hayek = *Gentianella anisodonta* (Borbás) A. et D. Löve
– – ssp. *pilosa* (Wettst.) Hayek = *Gentianella pilosa* (Wettst.) J. Holub
– *glauca* var. *major* (Ledeb.) = *Gentiana glauca* Pall.
– *halopetala* (A. Gray) T. Holm = *Gentianopsis halopetala* (A. Gray) Iltis
– *heterostemon* H. Smith = *Gentiana pedicillata* (D. Don) Griseb.
– *hopei* hort. = *Gentiana trichotoma* Kusn.
– *horomuiensis* Kudo = *Gentiana triflora* var. *horomuiensis* (Kudo) Hara
– *humilis* Stev. = *Gentiana aquatica* L.
– *imbricata* Froel. = *Gentiana terglouensis* Hacq.
– *jesoana* Nakai = *Gentiana triflora* var. japonica (Kusn.) Hara
– *igarashii* Miyabe et Kudo = *Gentiana algida* f. *igarashii* (Miyabe et Kudo) Toyokumi
– *karelinii* Griseb. = *Gentiana aquatica* var. *karelinii* Clarke
– *kawakamii* (Makino) Makino = *Gentiana jamesii* Hemsl.

– *kesselringii* Regel = *Gentiana walujewii* Regel et Schmalb. var. *kesselringii* (Regel) Kusn.
– *kochiana* Perr. et Song. = *Gentiana acaulis* L. s. str.
– *lacimata* Kit. = *Gentiana pyrenaica* L.
– *lagodechiana* hort. = *Gentiana septemfida* Pall. var. *lagodechiana* Kusn.
– *lutescens* Velen. = *Gentianella lutescens* (Velen.) J. Holub
– *makinoi* Lév. et Van non Kusn. = *Gentiana nipponica* Maxim.
– *menziesii* A. Gray = *Gentiana sceptrum* Griseb.
– *moorcroftiana* Wallich ex Griseb. = *Gentianella campestris* (L.) Börner
– *naitoana* Lév. et Faurie = *Gentiana triflora* var. *japonica* (Kusn.) Hara
– *nana* Wulfen = *Gentianella nana* (Wulfen) Pritchard
– *nipponica* var. *kawakamii* Makino = *Gentiana jamesii* Hemsl.
– *nipponica* var. *robusta* Hara = *Gentiana jamesii* var. *robusta* (Hara) Ohwi
– *nubigena* Edgew. = *Gentiana algida* Pall.
– *ochroleuca* Froel. = *Gentiana villosa* L.
– *orfordii* T. J. Howell = *Gentiana sceptrum* Griseb.
– *parvifolia* (Chapm.) Britt. = *Gentiana catesbaei* Walt.
– *phlogifolia* Schott et Kotschy = *Gentiana cruciata* L. ssp. *phlogifolia* (Schott et Kotschy) Tutin
– *pilos* Wettst. = *Gentianella pilosa* (Wettst.) J. Holub
– *plebeja* Cham. ex Bunge = *Gentianella amarella* (L.) Börner
– *porphyrio* J. F. Gmelin = *Gentiana autumnalis* L.
– *praecox* A. et J. Kerner = *Gentianella austriaca* (A. et J. Kerner) J. Holub
– *primulaefolia* Griseb = *Gentiana dilatata* Griseb.
– *procera* T. Holm = *Gentianopsis procera* (T. Holm) Ma
– *propinqua* Richardson = *Gentianella propinqua* (Richardson) J. M. Gillet
– *prostrata* Boiss. = *Gentiana aquatica* L.
– *puberula* Michx. = *Gentiana saponaria* L.
– *puberula* auct. not Michx. = *Gentiana puberulenta* Pringle
– *quadrifaria* Clarke = *Gentiana pedicillata* (D. Don) Wall. ex Griseb.
– *quinquefolia* L. = *Gentianella quinquefolia* (L.) Small
– *ramosa* Hegetschw. = *Gentianella ramosa* (Hegetschw.) J. Holub
– *rigescens* var. *japonica* Kusn. = *Gentiana triflora* var. *japonica* (Kusn.) Hara
– *romanzovii* Ledeb. ex Bunge = *Gentiana algida* Pall.
– *saxatilis* (Honda) Honda = *Gentiana scabra* var. *buergeri* (Miq.) Maxim.

– *scabra* var. *buergeri* f. *angustifolia* Kusn. = *Gentiana scabra* var *buergeri* f. *stenophylla* (Hara) Toyokumi
– *scabra* var. *buergeri* subvar. *saxatilis* Honda = *Gentiana scabra* var. *buergeri* (Miq.) Maxim.
– *scabra* var. *intermedia* Kusn. = *Gentiana scabra* var. *buergeri* (Miq.) Maxim.
– *scabra* var. *stenophylla* = *Gentiana scabra* var. *buergeri* f. *stenophylla* (Hara) Toyokumi
– *sceptrum* hort. non Griseb. = *Gentiana septemfida* Pall. var. *lagodechiana* Kusn.
– *stylophora* C. B. Clarke = *Megacodon stylophorus* (C. B. Clarke) Harry Smith
– *subpetiolata* Honda = *Gentiana scabra* var. *buergeri* (Miq.) Maxim.
– *tenella* Rottb. = *Gentianella tenella* (Rottb.) Börner
– *thermalis* O. Kuntze = *Gentianopsis* thermalis (O. Kuntze) Iltis
– *uliginosa* Willd. = *Gentianella uliginosa* (Willd.) Börner
– *verna* var. *alata* Griseb. = *Gentiana verna* var. *angulosa* Wahlenb.
– *verna* var. *favratii* Rittener = *Gentiana brachyphylla* Vill. ssp. *favratii* (Ritt.) Tutin
Hippion vernum (L.) F. W. Schmidt = *Gentiana verna* L.
Kudoa yakushimensis (Makino) Masum. = *Gentiana yakushimensis* Makino
Pneumonanthe affinis (Griseb.) Greene = *Gentiana affinish* Griseb.
– *andrewsii* (Griseb.) W. A. Weber = *Gentiana andrewsii* Griseb.
– *asclepiadea* Schmidt = *Gentiana asclepiadea* L.
– *calycosa* (Griseb.) Greene = *Gentiana calycosa Griseb.*

Not all the above species are described in detail in this book, since many of them, especially those belonging to the genus *Gentianella*, are of little or no garden merit. However, the list may be of help in solving problems of nomenclature.

Cultivation of gentians and their garden value

1. Cultivation practically impossible:
   Gentiana nivalis
   Gentianopsis ciliata

2. Cultivation feasible but difficult:
Gentiana bavarica
– *montana*
– *pyrenaica*
– *rostanii*
– *stragulata*
– *trichotoma*
– *tubiflora*
– *waltonii*

3. Can be successfully cultivated provided the requirements of each species are met, in particular adequate moisture during the growing period:
Gentiana calycosa
– *corymbifera*
– *farreri*
– *hexaphylla*
– *kurroo*
– *loderi*
Gentianopsis crinita
– *detonsa*
– *ornata*
– *parryi*
– *prolata*
– *veitchiorum*
– *verna*

4. Easily cultivated, given suitable soil and situation. Hybrids of the Asiatic autumn-flowering gentians:
Gentiana andrewsii
– *angustifolia*
– *clusii*
– *cruciata*
– *decumbens*
– *dinarica*
– *freyniana*
– *lutea*
– *pneumonanthe*
– *przewalskii*
– *scabra*
– *sceptrum*
– *sino ornata*

5. Easily cultivated in a moist, shady place:
Gentiana asclepiadea
– *saponaria*

6. Easily cultivated given the necessary minimum of moisture:
Gentiana septemfida and varieties

7. Easily cultivated provided their needs are met, but often shy flowering:
Gentiana acaulis (true species)
– *alpina*

8. Easily cultivated, but of no great beauty:
Gentiana cruciata ssp. *phlogifolia*
– *grombczewskii*
– *straminea*
– *tibetica*
– *walujewii* var. *kesselringii*

Conditions required by various gentians

1. Gentians for lime-free soil:
Gentiana affinis

– *amoena*	– *oregana*
– *austromontana*	– *ornata*
– *bisetaea*	– *ornata* var. *congestifolia*
– *cachemirica*	– *parryi*
– *corymbifera*	– *pneumonanthe*
– *frigida*	– *punctata*
– *gilvostriata*	– *purpurea*
– *hexaphylla*	– *saponaria*
– *jesoana*	– *sceptrum*
– *ishizuchii*	– *setigera*
– *linearis*	– *sino ornata*
– *loderi*	– *triflora* and varieties
– *makinoi*	– *veitchiorum*
– *newberryi*	

2. Lime-loving gentians:
Gentiana angustifolia

– *bavarica*	– *froelichii*
– *brachyphylla*	– *ligustica*
– *clusii*	– *occidentalis*
– *dinarica*	– *pumila*
– × *favratii*	– *terglouensis*

3. Full sun and adequate moisture:
All species of the *acaulis* group
Gentiana affinis

– *cachemirica*	– *saxosa*
– *puberulenta*	– *septemfida*

4. Cool moist places:
Gentiana andrewsii

– *asclepiadea*	– *platypetala*
– *autumnalis*	– *pneumonanthe*
– *calycosa*	– *saponaria*
– *decora*	– *sceptrum*
– *glauca*	– *makinoi*
– *linearis*	

In warm gardens in large towns, these species are difficult to keep. Yet there are many gardens in regions which enjoy higher atmospheric humidity, in the mountains at intermediate altitudes, in damp valleys, beside rivers or streams, and in the pre-alpine zone, where these species grow vigorously and flourish. They do best in a place where they have plenty of light but are shaded from the burning midday sun. The soil must of course meet their requirements, especially as regards pH.

5. Species which require half shade:
   Gentiana alba
   – *asclepiadea*
   – *clausa*
   – *glauca*
   – *saponaria*
   – *villosa*

6. Species for heavier, loamy soils; will not tolerate stagnant moisture:
Trumpet gentian species and hybrids
   Gentiana asclepiadea
   – *cruciata*
   – *lutea*
   – *pneumonanthe*
   – *punctata*
   – *septemfida*
   – *tibetica*

7. Species which flourish in sandy soils:
   Gentiana pumila
   – *saxosa*
   – *septemfida* var. *lagodechiana*
   – *verna* var. *angulosa*

Uses of gentians in the garden

1. For larger rock gardens only:
   Gentiana asclepiadea
   – *lutea*
   – 'Royal Blue'
   – *purpurea*
   Megacodon stylophora (syn. *Gentiana stylophora*)

2. Rock garden—a selection for beginners:
Trumpet gentian hybrids and forms such as

'Coelestina'
'Gedanensis'
'Holzmannii'
'Maxima'
'Saturn' etc.

Gentiana 'Angustifolia-Hybrids Frei'
– *clusii*
– *cruciata*
– – ssp. *phlogifolia*
– *dahurica*
– *dinarica*
– *farreri*
– *fetisowii*
– *gracilipes*
– × *hascombensis*

G. scabra var. *saxatilis*
– *septemfida*
–– 'Doeringiana'
–– var. *lagodechiana*
– *sino ornata*
– *tibetica*

Note: for British conditions this might be considered an adequate small list:

G. acaulis and its many forms.
G. × *macaulayi*
G. Septemfida
G. sino ornata

Hybrids of the Asiatic autumn-flowering gentians, provided their requirements can be met.

3. Rock gardens—a selection for the experienced grower:
Gentiana acaulis (syn. *G. kochiana*)
– *alpina*
– *bavarica*
–– var. *subacaulis*
– *brachyphylla*
– *prolata*
– *pyrenaica*
– *stragulata*
– *veitchiorum*
– *verna*
– *verna* var. *angulosa*
–– var. *oschtenica*
– *yakusimensis*

4. Rock gardens, under scree conditions
(provided soil pH requirements are met):
Gentiana bavarica
– *bellidifolia*
– *brachyphylla*
– *cachemirica*
– *pumila*
– *pyrenaica*
– *saxosa*
– *verna*

5. Gentians for troughs:

Gentiana algida	
– *angustifolia*	– *newberryi*
– *bellidifolia*	– *pumila*
– *dinarica*	– *saxosa*
– *farreri*	– *septemfida*
– *gelida*	– *verna*
– × *hascombensis*	–– var. *angulosa*
	–– var. *oschtenica*

Hybrids of the Asiatic autumn-flowering gentians.

There are various gentian species ideally suited for planting in troughs, though very few will tolerate full sun. However, in the writer's garden the following species have survived for several years in troughs in full sun:

Gentiana angustifolia
– *gelida*
– *septemfida*

For other species light shade is preferable or even a totally sunless position. The overall situation of the garden is the crucial factor. In a valley bottom where the evening mist gathers early, gentians will tolerate a sunnier position than they would in a garden situated on a south-facing slope. In dry weather the trough must be watered every day, though of course good drainage is essential.

6. Gentians for cut flowers:
Gentiana angustifolia and its hybrids
– *dinarica*
– *farreri*
– *triflora* var. *japonica* (syn. *G. jesoana*) = G. 'Royal Blue'
– *septemfida*
–– 'Doeringiana'
– *sino ornata* 'Praecox'

Various hybrids of Asiatic autumn-flowering gentians
Other long-stalked forms of the *acaulis* group

Apart from *Gentiana triflora* var. *japonica* (syn. *G. jesoana*) = G. 'Royal Blue', which furnishes long-stemmed flowers, the others are suitable only for small bouquets and flower arrangements. There are of course many other gentian species which the enthusiast can utilise for little posies and bouquets.

7. The best autumn-flowering gentians:
(compiled by Jim Jermyn for British and American readers)

G. × 'Angel's Wings'	'Kingfisher'
G. × 'Blue Bonnets'	*G.* × 'Mary Lyle'
G. × 'Carolii'	*G.* × stevenagensis
G. × 'Inverleith'	'Frank Barker'
G. × macaulayi	*G.* × 'Susan Jane'

Chromosome numbers:

Gentiana acaulis 2 n = 36	– *nivalis* 2 n = 14
– *alpina* 2 n = 36	– *pannonica* 2n = 40
– *asclepiadea* 2 n = 36	– *pneumonanthe* 2n = 26
– *bavarica* 2 n = 30	– *prostrata* 2 n = 26
– *brachyphylla* 2 n = 28	– *pumila* 2 n = 20
– *burseri* 2 n = 40	– *punctata* 2 n = 40
– *clusii* 2 n = 36	– *purpurea* 2 n = 40
– *cruciata* 2 n = 52	– *pyrenaica* 2 n = 26
– *dinarica* 2 n = 36	– *rostanii* 2 n = 30
– *frigida* 2 n = 24	– *terglouensis* 2 n = 40
– *froelichii* 2 n = 42	– *verna* 2 n = 28
– *lutea* 2 n = 40	

Suppliers of gentian seeds

UK

Jack Drake
Inshriach Alpine Plan Nursery
Aviemore
Inverness-shire PH22 1QS *Offers some rare varieties*

New Zealand
Southern Seeds
The Vicarage
Sheffield
Canterbury *New Zealand gentian varieties*

USA

Maver Rare Perennial Nursery
PO Box 18754
Seattle, WA 98118 *Special collections*

Suppliers of plants

UK

Ballalheannagh Gardens
Glen Roy
Lonnan
Isle of Man — *Standard varieties*

Jack Drake
Inshriach Alpine Nurseries
Aviemore
Inverness-shire PH22 1QS — *Rare and Chinese autumn-flowering varieties*

Edrom Nurseries
Coldingham
Eyemouth
Berwickshire TD14 5TZ — *Rare varieties*

Hartside Nursery Garden
Gill House
Alston
Cumbria CA9 3BL — *Wide selection*

Holden Clough Nursery
Holden
Bolton-by-Bowland
Clitheroe
Lancs BB7 4PF

W. E. Th. Ingwersen Ltd
Birch Farm Nursery
Gravetye
East Grinstead
West Sussex RH19 4LE

Reginald Kaye Ltd
Waithman Nurseries
Silverdale
Carnforth
Lancs LA5 OTY

Potterton and Martin
The Cottage Nursery
Moortown Road
Nettleton Caistor
Lincs LN7 6HX

USA

Maver Rare Perennial Nursery
PO Box 18754
Seattle, WA 98118 *No dispatch overseas*

Specialist Amateur Societies for the Growing of Gentians

(Note: addresses for amateur societies may change; those given below are correct for 1990)

UK

Alpine Garden Society
The Secretary
Lye End Link
St John's
Woking
Surrey GU21 1SW

Scottish Rock Garden Club
The Secretary
21 Erchiston Park
Edinburgh EH10 4PW

USA & Canada

American Rock Garden Society
Secretary: Buffy Parker
15 Fairmead Road
Darien, CT 06820 USA

Vancouver Island Rock &
Alpine Garden Society
Secretary: PO Box 6507
Station C
Victoria BC Y8P 5M4, Canada

Garden Club of BC
President: Mr Jim Babchuck
24128 56th Ave
RR 13 Langley
BC, Canada
Secretary: Mrs Kathi Leihsman
620 King George Way
West Vancouver, BC V7S 153

References

Bartlett, Mary: *Gentians*, Alpha Books, London, 1981
Berry, Grimshaw Heyes: *Gentians in the Garden*, Faber & Faber, London 1951
Budd, A. C.: *Budd's Flora of the Canadian Prairie Provinces*, revised and enlarged by J. Looman and K. F. Best, Research Branch Agriculture Canada, Ottawa 1981
Everett, T. H.: *The New York Botanic Garden Encyclopaedia of Horticulture*, Garland Publishing Inc., New York and London 1981
Heath, R. E.: *The Collingridge Guide to Collector's Alpines*, Collingridge, Richmond 1981
Hegi, G.: *Illustrierte Flora von Mitteleuropa*, vol. V, part 3, Parey, Berlin and Hamburg 1975
Hortus Third: *A Concise Dictionary of Plants Cultivated in the United States and Canada*, Collier Macmillan Publishers, London 1976
Ingwersen, Will.: *Ingwersen's Manual of Alpine Plants*, Will Ingwersen and Dunnsprint, Eastbourne 1978
Jelitto L., Schacht W. (eds.): *Die Freiland-Schmuckstauden*, vols. 1 and 2, Ulmer, Stuttgart 1963, 1966
——Schacht W., Fessler, A. (eds): *Die Freiland-Schmuckstauden*, Ulmer, Stuttgart 1985, 3rd edn
Journal of the Royal Horticultural Society, vol. LVII, part 2, London 1932
Köhlein, F.: *Pflanzen vermehren*, Ulmer, Stuttgart 1980, 6th edn
Mark, A. F., Adams, N. M.: *New Zealand Alpine Plants*
Ohwi, Jisaboro: *Flora of Japan*, Smithonian Institution, Washington DC 1984
Philipson, W. R., Hearn D.: *Rock Garden Plants of the Southern Alps*, Merlin Press, London, 1965
Polunin, O., Stainton A.: *Flowers of the Himalaya*, Oxford University Press, Delhi 1984
Pringle, James S.: *Sectional and Subgeneric Names in Gentiana (Gentianaceae)*, privately printed, Dr James S. Pringle, Royal Botanical Gardens, Hamilton, Ontario, Canada 1978
——*Taxonomy and Distribution of Gentiana (Gentianaceae) in Mexico and Cental America*, I. Sect. and II. Sect, privately printed 1977 and 1979, Royal Botanical Gardens, Hamilton, Ontario, Canada.

—— *Taxonomy of Gentiana, Section Pneumonanthe, in eastern North America*, privately printed 1967, Royal Botanical Gardens, Hamilton, Ontario, Canada

Tutin, T. G. (ed.): *Flora Europaea* vol. 3, Cambridge University Press, Cambridge 1972

Wilkie D.: 'Gentians', *Country Life*, London 1936, 2nd ed 1950

Wocke, E.: *Kulturpraxis der Alpenpflanzen*, Nachdruck Otto Koeltz, Königstein Taunus 1977

Zander: *Handwörterbuch der Pflanzennamen*, revised by F. Encke, G. Buchheim, S. Seybold. Ulmer, Stuttgart 1984, 13th edn

Catalogues of various alpine plant nurseries, notably Jac. Eschmann, Emmen, Switzerland

Acknowledgements of illustrations

Michio Cozuca, Japan: p. 78, middle right and below right. Hermann Fuchs, Hof: p. 23 above left, p. 41 middle left and right, p. 42 below, p. 59 middle right, p. 77 below left, p. 78 above right and middle left, p. 113 above left, above right and middle left, p. 114 above, and dust-jacket photo. Dieter Schacht, Munich: p. 24 below, p. 41 below left, p. 59 above right and below right, p. 60 middle right and below right, p. 77 above left, p. 95 above left. p. 114 below left. Wilhelm Schacht, Frasdorf: p. 59 middle left and below left, p. 60 below left, p. 77 below right, p. 114 below left.
The other colour photographs were taken by the author.

Index

Note page numbers in *italics* refer to illustrations.